Business Ethics: A Conversation

Second Edition

George Roe

BVT Publishing

Custom Publishing Division

Loose-Leaf ISBN: 978-1-62751-690-7
Softcover ISBN: 978-1-62751-691-4

BR072015SE

ACKNOWLEDGEMENTS

I would like to gratefully acknowledge the very insightful comments provided to me by Peter Thompson, PhD, of the University of Illinois at Chicago and William Ricketts, MA, MSA, both of whom spent a great deal of their time reviewing my initial drafts of this book.

I would also like to acknowledge the encouragement that I received from my students at the University of Illinois at Chicago. Every semester they have patiently sat through my Ethics classes and listened to me express my less than full satisfaction with the course books used in the class. And every semester they have said the same thing: if I did not like the books that are out there, write my own. Alright, I did, and this is it. Thanks to you all.

Last, I would like to acknowledge my wife, Helen. She has put up with me for over twenty years and has never failed to encourage me in whatever venture upon which I have embarked. I could not have done it without her.

ABOUT THE AUTHOR

George Roe's background has the unusual mix of both practical business experience and academic ethical theory. He has worked as a practicing lawyer, a former chief executive officer of two corporations, managing director of a private equity group, has served on various boards of directors, was a member of the Illinois CPA Society's Committee on Ethics, and a panel trustee in Federal Bankruptcy for the Northern District of Illinois. This experience has enabled George to bring both the theoretical and the practical aspects of business to his students. As an academic with over thirty years at the University of Illinois at Chicago, and Director of Ethics for the College of Business Administration, Professor Roe has integrated his years of practical experience into the classroom. He both designed and teaches the courses in Business Ethics to both graduate and undergraduate business students. He has won virtually every teaching award that the University and College have to offer.

Professor Roe is the author of numerous publications as well as a frequent television and print media resource for various issues in business ethics. He has been cited in print media ranging from The Chicago Tribune and Crain's Chicago Business to newspapers from Florida to Texas. He is a member of the Society for Business Ethics. He holds a BA degree from Marquette University in Philosophy and a Law Degree from DePaul University.

CONTENTS

CHAPTER ONE   Introduction..**1**
   1.1 Why Are We Doing This? 1
   1.2 So What Then Is Ethics? 2
   1.3 Welcome to Ethics 8

CHAPTER TWO   Critical Thinking **11**
   2.1 Introduction 11
   2.2 What Do We Mean By Critical Thinking? 11
   2.3 Thinking Logically—Empirical Evidence 13
   2.4 Thinking Logically—The Logic Itself 14
   2.5 Logical Fallacies 15
   2.6 Rationalizations 22

CHAPTER THREE   Ethical Theory and Business **29**
   3.1 Introduction 29
   3.2 Ethical Relativism 30
   3.3 Egoistic Ethics 31
   3.4 Kantian (Deontological) Ethics 32
   3.5 Utilitarian Ethics 34
   3.6 Deistic Ethics 35
   3.7 The Ethics of Care 35
   3.8 Virtue Ethics 36

CHAPTER FOUR   The Decision Making Process **41**
   4.1 Introduction 41
   4.2 The Process 42
   4.3 Why We Do The Wrong Thing 46
   4.4 A Question of Values 46
   4.5 The Fraud Triangle 47

CHAPTER FIVE   Corporate Social Responsibility...................**51**
   5.1 Introduction 51
   5.2 What is a Corporation? 51
   5.3 What is the Role of a Corporation? 52
   5.4 The Shareholder View of Corporations 52
   5.5 The Stakeholder View of Corporations 54
   5.6 The Reality View... 56

5.7 Social Responsibility... 57

5.8 Responsibility for Corporate Wrongdoing 58

CHAPTER SIX   Corporate Governance and Ethical Leadership........... 61

6.1 Introduction.. 61

6.2 Duty of Obedience... 62

6.3 Duty of Loyalty 63

6.4 Duty of Care.. 64

6.5 Ethical Leadership 64

6.6 The Seven Principles for Corporate Conduct.................................. 65

CHAPTER SEVEN   Moral Rights in the Workplace 73

7.1 Introduction 73

7.2 Right to Work... 74

7.3 Employment at Will.. 76

7.4 Contract Rights... 79

7.5 Health and Safety 81

7.6 Do You Have a Right to Privacy in the Workplace? 82

CHAPTER EIGHT   Diversity and Discrimination 87

8.1 Introduction.. 87

8.2 Affirmative Action.. 88

8.3 Preferential Hiring 89

8.4 Sexual Harassment 94

CHAPTER NINE   Ethics in a Global Environment............................. 101

9.1 Introduction... 101

9.2 Bribery of Foreign Officials... 102

9.3 The Foreign Corrupt Practices Act 103

9.4 Inter-Company Bribes... 106

CHAPTER ONE

Introduction

1.1 WHY ARE WE DOING THIS?

Welcome to Business Ethics. Of all the books that you could be reading right now, I am sure that this one was your first choice. Well, maybe I don't believe that either. So why are you reading this book? If the reason is that this is part of an ethics course requirement, that goes to the next question of why should you be taking a formal course in ethics to begin with? I mean you're already an ethical person, right? You probably can't remember the last time you robbed a gas station. So isn't this just another "feel good" course on which to waste your time? As you might guess I am going to say, no it isn't.

As you go through this course, hopefully, you will find that robbing gas stations isn't something that we worry a lot about in here. Instead, what we look to do in this course is to expose you to the many different types of ethical situations, *ethical dilemmas,* that you as a business student are going to encounter once you graduate and "are out there". What we look to accomplish in a course like this is to help create an attitude, a disposition, and a habit of living an ethical life in business. By attitude I mean an active state of awareness of the ethical issues that will surround you. If you don't know that there's an ethical problem to begin with, you're probably not going to deal with that problem very well. By disposition, I mean a general personal outlook, a temperament, to act in an ethical manner as a first choice, not as a last choice when all else has failed. Finally, by habit, hopefully as you progress throughout this course, your constant development of an ethical attitude and disposition will lead you to consistently, habitually, do the right thing, if for no other reason than just that, it is the right thing to do.

We will also be spending some time developing critical thinking skills. Every day someone is trying to sell us something. Be it a product, a politic or a philosophy, they will give us all sorts of arguments and reasons why they are right. More so, we do the same thing with ourselves. When we're not sure what to do in a particular situation, we argue with ourselves. We give ourselves various reasons as to why we should or should not do something. Are we being honest with ourselves? Or is our reasoning flawed? Do we have the ability, the skill, to critically look at the arguments of others, or ourselves, and separate out the fact from the fiction? This is where critical thinking skills are needed, and hopefully, by the end of this course, you will have mastered many of them.

The title of this book, *Business Ethics: A Conversation,* gives you some idea as to how we are going to approach this subject. This book is not intended as a purely academic treatise on business ethics. Instead, our goal is to talk to each other; to have a conversation about ethics. Sometimes the conversation may be uncomfortable, but then ethics and comfort do not always go hand in hand. As our conversations progress, you will gain greater insight into the ethical problems facing business today, and how you, as a future business manager can and will deal with them. So read on, and join the conversation.

1.2 SO WHAT THEN IS ETHICS?

The Cambridge Dictionary of Philosophy defines ethics as "the philosophical study of morality." Although perhaps not the most useful definition in the world, it does bring out two concepts, ethics and morality. Although "on the street", these terms are often used interchangeably, the two are not the same. If ethics is the study of morality, what then is this morality that ethics is studying?

Morality concerns itself with the *standards* that a given society, group, or even an individual has in deciding what is good or bad, right or wrong. They can usually be easily identified by their brevity.

It is wrong to steal.

It is wrong to kill an innocent.

It is good to be honest.

It is good to tell the truth.

It is good to be just.

It is bad to cheat.

You get the idea. Moral standards are usually very broad and general in nature. They express a value to something in generally a descriptive manner: it is good to, or it is bad to, or it is right to, or it is wrong to do something. Where do we get our morality? It comes from two sources: external from ourselves and internal to ourselves.

First, let's address the external sources. For most, our first experience with morality comes at a very young age from our family. The standards that we are taught at a young age fall into two classes. The first class is prudential–standards that our parents taught us in order to protect us from various harms. Mom tells us not to touch the hot stove. Why? Because she is afraid that we might get it dirty? Well maybe, but more likely she wants us to know, to learn, that touching hot things can harm us. The same is true for not running onto the road, leaning out of a window, and the other thousand things that we learn as children to help assure that we live long enough to become an adult. The second class of standards deals with relationships with others— It's bad to hit your little brother or sister. It's wrong to lie to our parents. You must be respectful of your teachers. The rules of prudence are usually pretty straight forward, and we learn very quickly what happens when we don't follow those rules. However, the standards of relationships, of dealing with others and even our community are far more complicated. This is where the external sources of morality can go far beyond just the family. We are given a further education in moral standards from our schools, our religious organizations, and society at large. The standards communicated to us from these sources are often confusing if not straight out contradictory. We may be told from some external sources that greed is bad. That it is good and right to respect other people. Then we turn on the television. Now we may get the message that greed is good. That it is perfectly alright to use other people for our own ends, "as long as no one gets hurt". You may remember the joy, or for many the not so much joy of your high school years. "Fitting in" and being accepted by the group was supremely important and oftentimes put a lot of stress on some of the standards that we learned from our other sources. Many may remember doing or saying things that upon reflection we wish we had not done or said. We only did it to "fit in", to be "accepted". For most this need to be accepted and to fit in never really goes away, and it should come as no surprise that the same stress of fitting in, or being accepted by our peers, and especially our superiors, continues in our professional business life as well. How we deal with those stresses in business, where frankly the stakes can be much higher than when in school, will be the greatest challenge many will face.

The second source of our moral standards is internal—it comes from within ourselves. We are not simply an empty bucket that is filled with moral standards solely from the outside. We grow. We mature. We begin to take in all of our experiences in life to date, and through that maturation process, we may develop our own new moral standards and/or reject some of the standards that we otherwise have been given. We may find that the standards of both prudence and relationships that made sense and worked for us as a child or even as a young adult, don't always work so well in dealing with the complexities of having to make adult decisions, especially in the realms of relationships. I say "may" being aware that this does not always happen with everyone. However, for those who do reach this level of maturity, new and self-generated moral standards become a part of our lives.

So how does this maturation process work? There are several theories, but one of the most commonly cited studies of this maturation process is by Lawrence Kohlberg and his stages of moral development.[1] The theory holds that moral reasoning, the basis for ethical behavior, has six identifiable developmental stages, which develop for most throughout their lives. The following is the situation that Kohlberg gives us.

The Heinz Dilemma

"In Europe, a woman was near death from a special kind of cancer. There was one drug that the doctors thought might save her. It was a form of radium that a druggist in the same town had recently discovered. The drug was expensive to make, but the druggist was charging ten times what the drug cost him to make. He paid $200 for the radium and charged $2,000 for a small dose of the drug.

"The sick woman's husband, Heinz, went to everyone he knew to borrow the money, but he could only get together about $1,000 which is half of what it cost. He told the druggist that his wife was dying and asked him to sell it cheaper or let him pay later. But the druggist said: "No, I discovered the drug and I'm going to make money from it." So Heinz got desperate and broke into the man's store to steal the drug for his wife. Should the husband have done that?" (Kohlberg, 1963).

Before reading on, stop for a moment and decide this case on your own. What would you have done? If Heinz had come to you for advice, what would you tell him? Should he break into the store and steal the drug or, simply put, let his wife die?

For Kohlberg this was not a right or wrong type of test. Instead, he wanted to understand the reasoning or each respondent's answer. He then took those responses and classified them into his stages of moral development. Here is his breakdown.

Level 1. Preconventional Morality

- **Stage 1. Obedience and Punishment**
  This is the earliest stage of moral development. This is what we expect from the youngest of children, which is not to say that the same is not found in some of the oldest of adults. At this stage, everything is about rules. They are fixed and absolute. Why must you obey these rules? Because if you don't, *you will face some form of punishment,* and punishment is like pain, and as has been observed by many, pain hurts.
- **Stage 2. Individualism and Exchange**
  At this stage of moral development, the child goes beyond the strict adherence to a rule because, well it's the rule. Now the child looks at the rules *in so far as it is in his or her self-interest.* Unlike the first stage above, which does not even consider other people, this stage does. There can even be a sense of reciprocity between people as long as that reciprocity serves your own self-interest.

---

1 Kohlberg, L. & Turiel, E. (1971). Moral development and moral education. In G. Lesser, ed. *Psychology and educational practice.* Scott Foresman.

Level 2. Conventional Morality

- **Stage 3. Interpersonal Relationships**
  This one may sound familiar from what we have already talked about. It is often called the "good boy-good girl" orientation. Remember our reference earlier to our high school days? Here our moral development is focused *on living up to the social expectations of others*. The emphasis is on conformity, on being "nice," or at least appearing to others as nice. Our actions are determined by how we think others are going to react to them in how they see us.
- **Stage 4. Maintaining Social Order**
  At this stage of moral development, people begin to consider society as a whole when making decisions. There is an awareness that the person is part of a larger world than just themselves or their narrow circle of relationships. This awareness of a greater society shifts one's focus to now *emphasizing the importance of maintaining law and order* by following the rules, by doing one's duty and respecting authority.

Level 3. Postconventional Morality

- **Stage 5. Social Contract and Individual Rights**
  At this stage, people begin to recognize that there may be a difference in values, beliefs and opinions held by others. This, unlike the previous stage where the rules for law and order come down from some authority, *the person now accepts the importance of rules, but only those rules that the members of society as a whole agree upon,* at least as far as this is practicable.
- **Stage 6. Universal Principles**
  This is Kohlberg's final stage of moral reasoning. It now introduces the idea that there can be universal ethical principles and they can be determined through abstract reasoning. At this stage, *the person may discover and follow internalized principles of justice,* even if they conflict with laws and rules.

What were the results of Kohlberg's study? As summarized in part by WC Crain[2], they are as follows:

Level I. Preconventional Morality

Stage 1. Obedience and Punishment   To the Heinz dilemma, the child typically says that Heinz was wrong to steal the drug because "It's against the law," or "It's bad to steal," as if this were all there was to it. When asked to elaborate, the child usually responds in terms of the consequences involved, explaining that stealing is bad "because you'll get punished" (Kohlberg, 1958b).

Although the vast majority of children at stage 1 oppose Heinz's theft, it is still possible for a child to support the action and still employ stage 1 reasoning. For example, a child might say, "Heinz can steal it because he asked first, and it's not like

---

2 W.C. Crain. (1985). *Theories of Development*. Prentice-Hall. pp. 118-136.

he stole something big; he won't get punished." Even though the child agrees with Heinz's action, the reasoning is still stage 1; the concern is with what authorities permit and punish.

Stage 2. Individualism and Exchange   At this stage children recognize that there is not just one right view that is handed down by the authorities. Different individuals have different viewpoints. "Heinz," they might point out, "might think it's right to take the drug, the druggist would not." Since everything is *relative,* each person is free to pursue his or her *individual* interests. One boy said that Heinz might steal the drug if he wanted his wife to live, but that he doesn't have to if he wants to marry someone younger and better-looking (Kohlberg, 1963, p. 24). What is right for Heinz, then, is what meets his own self-interests.

Level II. Conventional Morality

Stage 3. Interpersonal Relationships   At this stage children—who are by now usually entering their teens—see morality as more than simple propositions. They believe that people should live up to the expectations of the family and the community and behave in "good" ways. Good behavior means having good motives and interpersonal feelings such as love, empathy, trust, and concern for others. Heinz, they typically argued, was right to steal the drug because "He was a good man for wanting to save her," and "His intentions were good, that of saving the life of someone he loves." This answer deserves the label "conventional "morality" because it assumes that the entire community would share the attitude expressed—"anyone" would be right to do what Heinz did (Kohlberg, 1963, p. 25).

Stage 4. Maintaining the Social Order   Stage 3 reasoning works best in two-person relationships with family members or close friends, where one can make a real effort to get to know the other's feelings and needs and try to help. At stage 4, in contrast, the respondent becomes more broadly concerned with *society as a whole.* Now the emphasis is on obeying laws, respecting authority, and performing one's duties so that the social order is maintained. In response to the Heinz story, many subjects said they understand that Heinz's motives were good, but they cannot condone the theft. What would happen if we all started breaking the laws whenever we felt we had a good reason? The result would be chaos; society couldn't function.

Level III. Postconventional Morality

Stage 5. Social Contract and Individual Rights   At stage 4, people want to keep society functioning. However, a smoothly functioning society is not necessarily a good one. A totalitarian society might be well-organized, but it is hardly the moral ideal. At stage 5, people begin to ask, "What makes for a good society?" They begin to think about society in a very theoretical way, stepping back from their own society and considering the rights and values that a society ought to uphold. Stage 5 respondents basically believe that a good society is best conceived as a social contract into which people freely enter to work toward the benefit of all. They recognize that different social groups within a society will have different values, but they believe that all rational people would agree on two points. First, they would all want certain basic *rights,* such as liberty and life to be protected. Second, they would want some *democratic* procedures for changing unfair laws and for improving society.

In response to the Heinz dilemma, stage 5 respondents made it clear that they do not generally favor breaking laws; laws are social contracts that we agree to uphold until we can change them by democratic means. Nevertheless, the wife's right to live is a moral right that must be protected.

Stage 6: Universal Principles   Stage 5 respondents are working toward a conception of the good society. They suggest that we need to (a) protect certain individual rights and (b) settle disputes through democratic processes. However, democratic processes alone do not always result in outcomes that we intuitively sense as just. A majority, for example, may vote for a law that hinders a minority. Thus, Kohlberg believes that there must be a higher stage—stage 6—which defines the principles by which we achieve justice.

Kohlberg's conception of justice follows that of the philosophers Kant and Rawls, as well as great moral leaders such as Gandhi and Martin Luther King. According to these people, the principles of justice require us to treat the claims of all parties in an impartial manner, respecting the basic dignity of all people as individuals. The principles of justice are therefore universal; they apply to all. In actual practice, Kohlberg says, we can reach just decisions by looking at a situation through one another's eyes. If the druggist did this, even he would have recognized that life must take priority over property; for he wouldn't want to risk finding himself in the sick wife's shoes with property valued over life, especially his own life. Thus, they would all agree that the wife must be saved-this would be the fair solution.

So are you comfortable with this analysis? Would you conclude that the wife should be allowed to live? Be permitted to die? Live you say. All right. Why? Regardless of whether you would come to this decision because you feel that this is the "nice" thing to do, whether as part of the social contract the wife's right to life should be protected, or you feel this is a demand of justice, take your argument one step further. Consider the following.

You are now the CEO of a large publicly held pharmaceutical company. Over the years your company has spent millions of dollars developing a drug that treats a particularly nasty and oftentimes fatal disease. You are the only company with the legal rights to manufacture the drug, and there is no viable substitute available. You sell the drug worldwide; worldwide that is except in Africa. Why not there? Because the people needing the drug have no way of paying you for it. There are no insurance companies that can step in and no government sources that you can go to for payment. People are in fact dying for lack of your drug that would otherwise live. What do you do? Give it away free? Presume that this would result in a net loss for your company. How long do you think that could continue? Let's further presume that the drug, at least for now, is simply not available through normal means. Would someone in true need of the drug be justified in stealing it from whatever source is available? Would a black market in the drug be justified? Would a "rogue" pharmaceutical be justified in violating your patent to produce a generic version of your drug? Is Kohlberg useful to you here? Do you see any problems with Kohlberg's theory?

1.3 WELCOME TO ETHICS

In working your way through this problem, you are now in all likelihood entering the realm of ethics, not pure morality, not simply an application of standards. It is the role of ethics to *examine* those standards of morality and then decide if in any given situation they make sense. Are they reasonable? And here's the key to the process-reason. We use our reason *to make judgments.* We use our reason in deciding what our values are in life, either personally or professionally. It is a function of reason in deciding whether or not to take or not take a given action. We may do this by weighing and balancing the perceived costs of doing or not doing something over the perceived benefits of doing or not doing something. We use our reason in determining what the consequences may be of our actions, including those that may go far beyond how our decision merely affects ourselves. Lastly, and for our purposes in this course perhaps most importantly, it is our use of reason that helps us in resolving ethical dilemmas. We've use this term before. Now, let's define it.

There are a lot of definitions of what constitutes an ethical or moral dilemma (we now use these terms interchangeably). For example, a moral dilemma occurs when you are in a situation where you ought to do two things, but you can only do one. A famous example was given by the French philosopher Jean Paul Sartre, who considered the case of having a moral duty to go to Paris and take care of his sick mother, or join the Free French forces fighting the Nazis. Both actions ought to be done, but he could not do them both. This can get even harsher. What about the situation where you must do something, you must choose between two actions, and both of the choices produce a morally bad result. Recent stories about overseas sweatshops might be a good case in point. Most would agree that using child labor is wrong. You find that your company employs large numbers of children in your plant in a developing third world country. You have a decision to make. If you decide to put an end to this practice, the child and in many cases the child's family may literally starve to death. If you decide to allow the practice to continue, you are participating in a practice that most, probably including yourself, would consider unethical. In other words, no matter what decision you make, you are not going to be happy with the result. Dilemmas are a part of life. We experience them in our personal lives as well as in our business lives. The hard truth of the matter is that when faced with a true moral dilemma, regardless of the choice that you make, you are never going to go home at the end of the day feeling very good about the outcome. Someone is going to get hurt. Some otherwise good and valid moral standard is going to be violated for the sake of some other good and valid moral standard. Does this mean that you are ultimately in a "no win" situation? Yes, it does.

Let's go back and take a look at our pharmaceutical company and the Africa problem. On the one hand, there is the obvious temptation to say that life is more important than profits. Thus, the ethical and moral thing to do is to give the drug away to all those who need it and can't afford it. You are recognizing a moral standard of society to value life over property. On the other hand, if you do this, and in a worst-case scenario, the company goes broke, you and your investors lose everything, and your company will no longer be able to provide new and lifesaving drugs to others. Here you recognize a moral standard of loyalty to your investors, and perhaps a moral duty to future people who would otherwise be deprived of the benefit of your future drug research. Presume you can't do both but must choose one. What do you do?

These are the types of questions that you will be dealing with throughout this course. It doesn't matter what your business major is. Each area of business has its own ethical challenges. We will be looking at the various problems you can, and for most of you, will be facing as you go about your careers. It is hoped that by the time we are done, you will be able to recognize the ethical challenges you will face and have developed the critical reasoning skills needed to deal with those challenges.

1.4 CHAPTER HIGHLIGHTS

1. What is the purpose of this course?

The purpose of this course is to help create an attitude, a disposition, and a habit of living an ethical life in business.

2. What do we mean by morality?

Morality concerns itself with the *standards* that a given society, group, or even an individual has in deciding what is good or bad, right or wrong.

3. Where do we get our morality?

It comes from two sources: external from ourselves and internal to ourselves.

4. What are the two classes of morality that we generally learn from our family at a young age?

The first is prudential. This means the standards that our parents taught us to protect us from various harms. The second class of standards deals with relationships with others.

5. What is one of the most commonly cited studies of the moral maturation process?

One of the most commonly cited studies of this maturation process is by Lawrence Kohlberg and his stages of moral development. The theory holds that moral reasoning, the basis for ethical behavior, has six identifiable developmental stages, which develop for most throughout their lives.

6. What is the role of ethics?

It is the role of ethics to *examine* standards of morality and then decide if in any given situation they make sense.

7. What is one definition of a moral dilemma?

A moral dilemma occurs when you are in a situation where you ought to do two things, but you can only do one.

8. What is another definition of a moral dilemma?

Some otherwise good and valid moral standard is going to be violated for the sake of some other good and valid moral standard.

PROBLEM FOR DISCUSSION

You are the chief executive officer of an emergency air medical company. When someone is critically injured, it is your company's business to send a medical helicopter with a licensed nurse and medic to the scene of the accident and transport the victim to the nearest hospital. Your medical personnel are licensed in the states that you do business. As circumstances would have it, one night your company receives a frantic call from a local sheriff's office telling you that there has been a terrible accident. A young woman crashed her car in a rural area, and was in critical condition. No ground ambulance could get to her in time, and the sheriff asks that you send your medical helicopter right away.

Now you have a problem. The sheriff in question was calling right over the state line from a state wherein you are not licensed to work. In fact, if you go to the scene and render medical assistance, you are violating the criminal law of that other state. As such, not only can your company be criminally charged and fined, you, as the CEO who authorized the flight might also have personal criminal liability. More so, even your medical personnel on board the helicopter, your nurse and medic, would also be committing a criminal act, as they are not licensed within that other state. There are no "good Samaritan" law exceptions in that other state and no other medical helicopter is available within that state. You tell the Sheriff you cannot go due to his state law, but the sheriff begs you to come anyway, telling you in no uncertain terms that this young woman is going to die unless you do something.[1]

You now have about two minutes to make your decision. Do you send your helicopter, or not? What are the ethical issues involved? How would Kohlberg look at this problem?

---

1 This case is based on an actual event.

CHAPTER TWO

Critical Thinking

2.1 INTRODUCTION

We are now going to spend a fair amount of time learning and practicing critical thinking skills. And make no mistake about it, these are indeed skills. And like any skill, they are learned, and are then only perfected through practice. In this chapter we are going to examine the skills you need to think critically. We are going to look at two issues in critical thinking: logical fallacies and rationalizations. We are all guilty of doing both, thinking illogically and rationalizing our actions when we are trying to justify the otherwise unjustifiable. As we learn to recognize both of these pitfalls, our ability to deal with others, as well ourselves, will improve dramatically.

2.2 WHAT DO WE MEAN BY CRITICAL THINKING?

There are a lot of definitions. One of the better ones comes from WG Sumner.

> [Critical thinking is] . . . the examination and test of propositions of any kind which are offered for acceptance, in order to find out whether they correspond to reality or not. The critical faculty is a product of

education and training. It is a mental habit and power. It is a prime condition of human welfare that men and women should be trained in it. It is our only guarantee against delusion, deception, superstition, and misapprehension of ourselves and our earthly circumstances.[1]

There are two important points to take-away from Sumner. First, critical thinking is a test of something. Someone tells you to buy some product because... and here you can insert any reason you want. Does that reason make sense? Does it, as Sumner says, correspond to reality? The only way that we may know is by looking at the arguments and/or evidence given in support of the sales pitch, and then we come to our own conclusion. Obviously this implies that there is some argument given, or that there is some evidence put forth in support of the proposition that we are being asked to accept. How many of us would buy a product because the salesman simply says he would like us to do so? How quick are we to vote for a given candidate if the candidate's only argument as to why we should vote for him or her is that he or she really wants the job? We need more. So for example, arguments such as "because that's how I feel", or "that's how I was taught" or "that's just the way I think" simply do not work. They are all devoid of any reason and are not evidence of anything. As we will see in a moment, critical thinking is reasonable thinking. It is not blind acceptance of any proposition that cannot be supported in reason or by the evidence.

Now, this takes us to the second take-away from Sumner. Why is it that we test propositions by reason and evidence? Because that "is our only guarantee against delusion, deception, superstition, and misapprehension of ourselves and our earthly circumstances." This is no small matter. Critical thinking is both our shield and our sword. As our shield, it protects us from those who would try to convince us to do something (buy a product, vote for a candidate, introduce a marketing program in our company, "re-state" our financials, etc.,) that upon any real critical analysis we otherwise would not do. However, critical thinking is also our sword. In both our business and personal lives, we are constantly arguing about something with someone. You want your professor to re-grade your exam. You want your significant other to go on vacation where you want to go. You have to present to your boss an argument as to why you deserve that pay raise. If most of us think back the last 24 to 48 hours or so, the odds are better than average that you tried to convince someone to do something. If you master critical thinking, the chances of you succeeding in this go up dramatically. And let's not forget the arguments we have with ourselves. If we subject ourselves to the same critical thinking analysis that we want to subject others, the odds of us making a better more reasoned decision increase. Here's a tip to decide if your critical thinking skills are in play. When you are asked "why" you want to do or not do something, can you articulate the reason with something better than "that's just the way I feel" or "I just want to?" If not, you have some more work to do.

I hope that I have convinced you of the importance of critical thinking. Now let's move on to the next part of the process, developing the skills themselves.

---

1 Sumner, W. G. (1940). *Folkways: A Study of the Sociological Importance of Usages, Manners, Customs, Mores, and Morals,* New York: Ginn and Co., pp. 632, 633.

2.3 THINKING LOGICALLY—EMPIRICAL EVIDENCE

How is it that we know that something is true, or at least believe it to be true? One way is through the observation of empirical evidence. Remember when Mom told you not to touch the hot stove? Did you listen? Probably not. So what happened? You touched it, and you got burned. What did you learn from this? Besides that you should listen to your mother, you also learned from empirical evidence that a hot stove can burn you. You probably then were able to deduce that a hot flame is like a hot stove. Touch it, and you can get burned. This is the funny thing about flames. How many of us have passed our hand through a flame to feel the heat? You discover every now and then that we still get burned, even though we know from past observations that a flame can hurt us. Did we do this because we didn't believe our past experience and observations? We thought that maybe this time we have a cold flame? Maybe, but probably not. We seem to want to continually test our past experiences, until we reach the point in our "experiments" where we are confident that the result isn't going to change: that all flames are hot and the only question left remaining in any given "flame case" is how hot.

The nice thing about empirical evidence is that we do not necessarily always have to be the tester. We oftentimes can and do rely upon the observations and conclusions of others that a given proposition is true because they, not us, have empirically tested it. They have actually seen it, felt it, or measured it themselves, and we are asked to accept their findings. For many things this works quite well, although remember that this always requires some leap of faith on our part. Simply stated, we are asked to believe what some other person tells us is true outside of our own actual experience. Could they be lying? Yes. Could they have misinterpreted or misunderstood their own evidence? Yes. But then again, we are subject to the same limitations in interpreting or understanding our own experience.

Things are not always what they appear to be. Galileo was laughed at because he thought that the earth revolved around the sun. At the time, people thought the man to be crazy. They might have said, "Galileo, look out your window. In the morning the sun is in the east and by the end of the day it is in the west. You can actually watch it revolve around the earth for yourself. What could be clearer?" As we know, Galileo was right, regardless of what appeared to empirically be true for most people who simply used their eyes. So what do we conclude from this? That one person's "fact" is another person's fantasy? Sometimes, but not always. This requires us to always maintain a level of healthy skepticism when others are trying to persuade us of the "facts of the matter." From the perspective of ethics, this becomes an even greater challenge. Ethical dilemmas don't happen in a vacuum. They always have surrounding facts. If we get our facts wrong, this may very well result in a conclusion that we may regret. But it's worse than that. In a fast moving ethical environment, where you have to make a decision now, not only may the facts not be what you thought they were, facts have a bad habit of changing as you are provided with more information. We will talk more about this in Chapter Four, the Decision Making Process. For now, work on that healthy skepticism when presented with facts, be they your facts or someone else's.

2.4 THINKING LOGICALLY—THE LOGIC ITSELF

A second way that we accept something as being true is because it is logical to do so. That is, the conclusion that we are asked to accept flows coherently from an agreed-upon fact or facts. For example, we might say that all dogs have four legs, and that Flash is a dog. Knowing that Flash is a dog, and that all dogs have four legs, we know that Flash must also have four legs.

Logical statements or arguments have premises and conclusions. The example above contains two premises: 1. All dogs have four legs, and 2. Flash is a dog. It has one conclusion: Flash has four legs. It is a logical argument because the conclusion flows naturally and coherently from the premises. At least that's how it's supposed to work.

People regularly make arguments that have a logical form, but none of the substance of logic; these arguments contain logical fallacies. Logical fallacies are commonplace, and they come in two basic forms. First, a logical fallacy occurs when one or all of the premises in an argument are either wrong or at least questionable. If we say that all four legged creatures are dogs, and that Flash has four legs, therefore Flash must be a dog, we would be making a fallacious argument because our primary premise, all four legged creatures are dogs, is incorrect. The conclusion does indeed flow from the premises, but one of the premises is faulty. And this example raises an interesting point: the fact that an argument is logically fallacious does not necessarily mean that the conclusion is wrong, only that the reasoning is poor. Flash may indeed be a dog, but if we truly know that, we must know it for some other reason than the fact that he has four legs. So it is possible to come to the right conclusion for the wrong reason. However, this is usually not the case. Most of the time a wrong premise will result in a wrong conclusion. Do you see where this takes us back to the problem of facts? It is not always easy to know if the premises being offered as true really are. Remember healthy skepticism? Keep working on it.

The second kind of logical fallacy occurs when the conclusion does not follow from the premises. If we say that all dogs have four legs, and that Flash is a dog, we can't conclude that Fluffy has four legs because the premises have given us no information about Fluffy, which may be your pet centipede.

Identifying these types of logical mistakes takes practice because they are not always obvious. Fortunately you have unlimited sources to go to for this practice. Turn on almost any commercial or political debate, read any blog, or eaves-drop on any conversation in your neighborhood pub and you will in all likelihood find many examples of faulty logic. The person who can tell the difference between the sound and the not so sound logic has a distinct advantage over all of those who cannot.

We are now going to take a look at some of the more common logical fallacies that you are likely to encounter in day-to-day life. Sometimes the logical flaw is obvious. However, many times it is not. The better you become at recognizing logical flaws in other people's arguments, the better equipped you will be with that shield and sword of critical thinking.

2.5 LOGICAL FALLACIES

So what are the tricks to the "art of persuasion?" What are some of the most common assaults on reason that every salesperson, every politician seems to have down pat and use every day to persuade you to do or not do something? The following is a sampling of some of the most common logical fallacies that we see every time we turn on the television. If you know these, and can recognize them when you hear them, in the words of Sumner, this will be your best guarantee "against delusion, deception, superstition, and misapprehension."

1. Appeal to False Authority

Try this. A number of years ago, Hall of Fame NFL quarterback Joe Namath endorsed Beautymist pantyhose. Now celebrities endorse various products all the time. From a marketing perspective, the message seems to be if you buy this product you too can be like...fill in the celebrity's name. Or, if the product is good enough for the celebrity it is good enough for you. Remember our discussion on logic? If we take this endorsement down to its logical elements, we would get the following:

Premises:

1. Joe Namath, NFL quarterback, thinks that Beautymist manufactures the best panty hose on the market.
2. Joe Namath is an authority on pantyhose.

Conclusion:

3. Beautymist panty hose are the best on the market.

Do you see anything wrong with this line of reasoning? Why would an athlete who neither wears nor designs pantyhose know anything about the pantyhose business? He wouldn't. The secondary premise is false. Namath presumably is not an expert on pantyhose. This is an appeal to false authority. This is not to say that appeals to authority are never valid. Of course they can be. For example, there is no reason to ignore Joe Namath's advice on the mechanics of throwing a football. You just want to be sure that the authority being cited as proof of the proposition is in fact a legitimate authority in the subject matter. Beware appeals to *false* authority. (And basketball great Michael Jordan on underwear?) You decide for yourself.

2. Red Herring—Evading the Issue

Tom is running for political office. A reporter interviewing him asks his opinion on what he would do about struggling European banks. Tom says, "That's a really great question. I believe that we must take all reasonable steps to stop the spread of nuclear weapons in the world."

Successful politicians from all points on the political spectrum tend to be masters of the red herring fallacy. This happens when someone tries to divert an argument or a question to an arguably related or even totally unrelated issue. You might ask a politician a question about gas prices, and he might give you a response whose substance is all about foreign policy. Most of the time this is done because the person being asked the question either doesn't know the answer and doesn't want to admit to that, or believes that if he does give the answer it won't be very well received. So when your professor asks you about depreciating assets, just say that you really believe this is the year the Cubs will win the World Series. Good luck with that.

This may sound like an easy fallacy to spot, but "good" red herrings can be tough to notice because the speaker may make what is an excellent, eloquent and absolutely valid point; it just happens to belong in a different argument. If the speaker is lucky, the questioner may get sidetracked and then ask about the topic that the speaker really wanted to talk about. If you want to hear more examples of this fallacy, just tune in to any Sunday morning political talk show or interviews that politicians give, and especially political debates, all are abundant sources of red herring fallacies.

3. Attacking the Person

You are on the Board of Directors of Megacorp. It has come to your attention that the company's CEO may have made some illegal payments to a foreign official to land a major contract. At the board meeting you specifically ask the CEO about these payments. He responds by saying that you are only asking this because you have never liked him and are looking to take his job. Any logic problems here?

This fallacy is extremely common. It is a special type of red herring. It evades the issue at hand, but does so in a very specific way: by attacking an opponent personally rather than his or her contentions. Whenever an argument shifts focus from the points of debate to the debaters themselves, it is likely that the argument has become fallacious.

4. False Dichotomies

Let's go back to Megacorp. The argument between you and the CEO is now very heated. The CEO turns to the other directors who seem to be uncertain as to what they should do, and he says, "Look. You are either for me or against me." Your response?

The statement, "You're either for me or against me" is a common example of a false dichotomy, or what some call a false choice. What makes it false? It presents only two absolute choices as the only two viable options in a given situation when in reality there is oftentimes at least one more option. False dichotomies are often nothing more than rhetorical blackmail, intended to convince a person to make a choice or take a position without examining all of the options available. Indeed, the speaker is saying that there are no other options. This is not to say that we can't conceive of a situation where in fact there is no other choice, but again, I recommend that you come to that decision very slowly. There usually are other options.

5. Fallacy of Complex Questions

The fallacy of complex questions is a special form of false dichotomy. Questions like "Have you stopped beating your dog?" "Have you gotten your shop lifting under control?" and "Have you given up being an intolerant bigot?" Each (in most situations) amounts to this form of false dichotomy. Can you see why? By answering "yes" to these questions, you seem to admit past abuse, theft or bigotry; by answering "no," you appear to be admitting to ongoing instances of the same. The question does not allow for a simple, direct and un-incriminating answer. You can find this sort of thing or its variation with interviews by some less than honorable journalists. Candidate Jones is running for a political office. The reporter asks him the following question, which has absolutely no basis in fact. "Mr. Jones, is it true that you embezzled money from you former employer?" Jones, looking surprised and having no idea where this question came from, says no, it is not true at all. Tomorrow's headline in the newspaper? "Jones denies embezzling money from past job!"

6. The Gambler's Fallacy

If you flip an evenly weighted coin twice, and it lands on heads both times, what are the odds that a third flip will land on tails? Any respectable statistician will tell you that the odds remain fifty-fifty. However, a person operating under the gambler's fallacy maintains that the odds are in favor of the coin landing on tails, as it has already landed on heads twice. The gambler's fallacy occurs when a person allows a separate and distinct past event to influence his beliefs regarding the outcome of a separate and distinct future event. The fact that the coin landed on heads twice before in no way affects the odds that the next flip will land on tails. So the next time that you are at the casino on the slot machine, which just took almost all of your money, you might not want to give it what little money you have left, saying to yourself, "It's got to be my turn to win." Presuming the game is not rigged; each "pull" has an equal chance of winning...or taking your money.

7. Argument by Threat

In 2005, the American Film Institute voted a line from *The Godfather* as one of the greatest quotes in the history of American film.[2] The line? "I'm going to make him an offer he can't refuse," referring to mafia boss Vito Corleone's habit of threatening people with violence in order to persuade them to his point of view.

Some people refer to this fallacy as an "appeal to the stick." Logically, a person shaking a stick at you is not necessarily making a logical argument for his position simply because he threatens to crack you over the head if you do not agree with him. Power does not make truth, and threats, while perhaps persuasive, are not logical arguments.

---

2 http://www.afi.com/Docs/tvevents/pdf/quotes100.pdf

8. Circular Arguments

A circular argument happens when the speaker presupposes the truth of the conclusion in the premises. Remember that the purpose of the premises is to give us reasons to ultimately accept the truth of the conclusion. In other words, if we have to assume that the conclusion is true in order to accept the truth of the premise, the argument is circular. The classic example of a circular argument is one given to prove the existence of God. It goes like this:

> The Bible says that God exists.
>
> God wrote the Bible.
>
> Therefore, God exists.

Do you see the problem? The second premise assumes that God exists which of course is what we are trying to prove in the conclusion. There may be many excellent arguments for the existence of God, but this is not one of them.

9. Reasoning from the Relative to the Absolute

This is a fallacy that we hear all the time. Sometimes it's really obvious. "Everyone named Mike is a no good drunk. At least the person I knew named Mike was." Although this may seem foolish on its face, this is one of the most common arguments used to justify bigotry and intolerance. We take an incredibly small sample, perhaps based on our own limited experience, and generalize it to include everyone or everything, or every place that bears any resemblance to that one or so limited person, thing or place. Thus, the fellow you knew named Mike might very well have been a no good drunk, but to therefore conclude that everyone else named Mike is the same, does not logically follow.

However, sometimes it's not that obvious. For example, a person says that it is always unethical to break the law. Why does he say this? He says this because he has never experienced a situation where it may be more ethical to break the law than to follow it. At first glance, this might seem completely reasonable. As a practical matter, most of us never really find ourselves in situations where doing something that is against the law is a better ethical choice than following the law. However, there may be situations where that might not be true, in which an illegal activity may not only be morally acceptable, it may be even morally preferable. How many of us would condemn aiding escape attempts by slaves in pre-Civil War America, which was illegal, as was hiding Jews in Nazi Germany? Not only would many of us say these actions are ethical, but also praiseworthy. We reason from the relative to the absolute when we observe something that is sometimes true and then claim that it always true.

10. Perception Is Reality

Remember Galileo? Again, this is probably the best example of people confusing their perception of what is true with what in fact may be true. If you ever have the chance to watch a good magic show, you will see how this works. There's the common magician's trick of sawing the lady in half. Now, you know that he really didn't do that, but when done right, it sure looks like he did. Illusion is the magician's stock in trade. Put another way, seeing should not always be the same as believing. This goes far beyond any magical entertainment value. In more serious circumstances people's lives and reputations can and have been ruined because "it sure looks like he's guilty" when all, or in some cases, very few of the facts are really known—simply because something looks like it is true does not necessarily make it true.

In the decision making process, this issue may be your greatest challenge. As we said above, facts have a bad habit of changing. From a practical standpoint, when you have to make a decision, oftentimes all you have to go on are the "facts" as you understand them to be at the time. My best advice? Remember our suggestion about keeping a healthy skepticism about you? That may be your best defense. Perception in fact does not always accurately represent reality.

11. Fallacy of Free Choice

Let's do a quick survey. How many of you are a) in favor of sweatshops, or b) not in favor of sweatshops? My instincts tell me that most choose choice b. So let's presume that sweatshops are a bad thing. Now, you find yourself in a company that has a factory in a very poor developing country. The workers there are paid two dollars a day. The working conditions are below anything that would be acceptable by U.S. standards. If you had it within your power, would you close that factory, presuming that it is not cost effective for your company to modernize the facility and pay a much higher US-similar wage? One side of the argument says no, those working there are there voluntarily and under their own free will. No one forced them to take the job, and if they don't like the pay or the working conditions, they can quit anytime they want. But is this really true? Is there really a free choice in the matter? How "voluntary" is a choice between a dangerous job with an extremely low wage and the real possibility of starving to death without that job? As a practical matter, to argue "free choice" is probably fallacious. Phrases such as "Nobody made them take that job" and similar lines, while technically true, lack any real substance as they often are masking a situation that lacks any real choice.

12. Confusing Legality with Morality

Although it is not my intent to pick on politicians, they are a really rich source of fuzzy if not straight out fallacious logic. On as fairly regular basis, some new scandal develops involving some politico. If direct denial of the accusations doesn't work, you will often hear the response, "I didn't break any laws" or "I did nothing illegal." The obvious point they are trying to make is that if I did not do anything illegal, I did nothing immoral. Do we buy this? A lot of people do. However, taking a more reasoned approach we may conclude that law and morality are not necessarily always related. Even a cursory knowledge of legal history tells us that law and morality are regularly at odds with each other. For example, slavery in parts of this country right up to the Civil War was perfectly legal. Would you, therefore, conclude that based on this fact alone, slavery was moral? How about Nazi Germany? Millions of Jews and others were put to death under the laws of Germany that also made this legal. Of course we like to believe that our laws are indeed moral and righteous, and most of the time they are. Unfortunately that is simply not always the case. The fact that something is legal does not make it moral, nor does the fact that something is illegal make it immoral. The moral and the legal are distinct realms, and they do not necessarily coincide.

13. Confusing Causation with Correlation

Confusing causation with correlation is one of the more troubling fallacies we encounter. Take the following argument. The local temperance league demonstrates that the vast majority of alcoholics had their first experience with alcohol by having a beer as their first drink. Thus, it is argued, that beer causes alcoholism. Do we agree? It might be argued that there is a *correlation* between drinking beer and becoming an alcoholic, but there is no evidence in the argument that drinking beer actually *causes* alcoholism. The argument confuses correlation with causation.

The reason that this is a most troubling fallacy is that it is not always clear as to whether the correlation is in fact causation. It very well may be. However, from a logical perspective, the speaker has to do more than just make the claim.

14. Fallacy of Small Numbers

Statistics can be powerful pieces of evidence in an argument. Unfortunately, like facts, numbers can be pretty slippery. Whenever anyone is trying to convince you of the truth of their position based on statistics, you are always well advised to look behind the numbers. For example, two people were walking down the street, each wearing brown shoes. A car hits one of them. Could I argue that based on my study of two individuals, people wearing brown shoes have a 50 percent chance of being run over by a car? Of course we would laugh at this. Why? Because the statistical sample is far too small to provide any meaningful conclusions. Thus, we have the fallacy of small numbers. This fallacy can be very hard to detect. The seller of a medication may claim that clinical tests showed that 60 percent of the subjects in the study benefited from the treatment. If we could look behind the numbers, we might find that the study consisted of ten people, and six of them worked for the seller. A pretty small and perhaps biased sample. And this presumes that we have the ability to look behind the curtain. Most often, statistics seem to be thrown out there for you to simply take as being true. So whether statistics are being intentionally "massaged" to deceive you, or are just a reflection of sloppy work, the end result may be the same. They point to a conclusion that is not supported in logical or factual evidence. The old adage is still true; "Numbers don't lie but liars use numbers."

15. Confusing Explanation with Justification

A common fallacy among people who have just acted unethically is to confuse explanation with justification. Jones is a defendant in a criminal case. He has been charged with multiple murders. When asked why he did these things, he (or his lawyer) explains that he had a terrible childhood, was addicted to drugs, and dropped out of school. This of course is being said in order to elicit sympathy for the defendant in hopes of a lighter punishment with the implication that it wasn't really all the defendant's fault. All of this may be true, but at best, it may be an explanation for his criminal acts. The explanation does not justify the acts. Simply put, your explanation may tell me why you did something despicable; It does not justify the despicable act itself.

16. Emotional Appeal

An appeal to emotion is a type of argument, which attempts to arouse the emotions of its audience in order to gain acceptance of its conclusion. Despite the example of Mr. Spock from the original *Star Trek* television series, emotion is not always out of place in logical thinking. However, there is no doubt that strong emotions can subvert rational thought, and playing upon emotions in an argument is often fallacious.

This is not to say that an appeal to someone's emotions is always inappropriate. The key is to understand why the appeal is being made. For example, no student would try to prove that one plus one equals three by playing upon the teacher's sympathy for the long hours of hard work the student put in to come to this conclusion. Such an appeal would be obviously irrelevant, since either the equation is correct or it is not, regardless of the student's best efforts. But consider this. What if the teacher tells the student that unless the student studies hard and attends all of the classes the student will get an F in the course. Instead of an appeal to sympathy tried by the student, the teacher is making an appeal to fear. In both cases, there is an appeal to emotion. The first is invalid, and the second, the teacher's, is valid. What is the difference? The first argument by the student was used to try and convince the teacher as to the truth of the matter, that one plus one equals three. It was used to try and influence the teacher's belief. The teacher's argument, on the other hand, was not intended to influence the student's belief in any particular proposition. Instead, it was used solely to motivate the student to work harder in the class by instilling fear of failing the course, which can be an excellent motivator.

So, one distinction between relevant and fallacious appeals to emotion is based on the distinction between arguments which aim to motivate us to action, and those which are intended to convince us to believe something. Appeals to emotion are always fallacious when intended to influence our beliefs, but they are sometimes reasonable when they aim to motivate us to act. Also, remember that the fact that we want something to be true on a deep emotional level does not in itself give us the slightest reason to believe that it is true, and the fact that we fear something being true is no reason to think it false.[3]

---

3 T. Edward Damer, *Attacking Faulty Reasoning: A Practical Guide to Fallacy-Free Arguments (Third Edition)* (Wadsworth, 1995), pp. 44-56. David Hackett Fischer, *Historians' Fallacies: Toward a Logic of Historical*

17. False Analogy

We all like to argue our point through analogy, through comparisons. The problem comes in when the two things that we are comparing, that we are saying are the same, really are not. Most of time we can spot these false analogies from their first premise or opening sentence.

Students are like nails. Just as nails must be hit in the head in order to make them work, so must students. Is this a valid analogy? The answer is yes only if you agree that in fact students are the same as nails. Most of us would probably conclude that is not the case.

Business is like a poker game and a large part of that game is to try to bluff and deceive the opponent. Agree? Not unless you believe that business is nothing more than a game.

If we can land a man on the moon we should be able to cure cancer. Are the two activities really the same? Probably not.

If we want to use an analogy, be sure that it is an "apples to apples" comparison. Comparing apples to light bulbs is usually a stretch.

18. Confusing Freedom of Speech/Religion with Truth

In our society we take great pride in our fundamental right to say what we want and to believe what we want, and that is how it should be. However, we must be careful not to confuse a person's right to say or believe whatever they want with the truth of the proposition. For example, a given person may say that he sincerely believes that the world is flat or one plus one equals three. It is his right to so speak and believe. However, simply put, he is wrong. But can we actually tell him he is wrong? After all, that's what he really believes. Not only can we tell him he is wrong, we may have an ethical duty to do so. What would our response be if a person said that he truly believed in a master race, and that all other inferior races should be eliminated? (There is precedent for this belief.) Can we tell him that his honest belief is wrong and at the same time acknowledge his right to believe the nonsense? Absolutely. Freedom to speak and believe something does not in itself prove the truth of anything. Don't misunderstand. What a person believes to be true may in fact be true. Only understand that the bear belief of the truth of the matter does not make it so.

All of the above may seem like a pretty long list. In fact, the list is a great deal longer. We've just looked a few of the more common types of fallacies, but if you can at least recognize these when you see or hear them, you will be one up step on the person on the other side of the argument.

2.6 RATIONALIZATIONS

Someone once asked what is the difference between a white lie and a rationalization. One answer is that we tell someone a white lie to make that other person feel better.

We tell ourselves a rationalization in order to make ourselves feel better. Why is it that we have to make ourselves feel better? Usually because we have done, or are thinking about doing something that we know in our hearts is wrong. More specifically, rationalizations are nothing more than our attempts to justify actions that we feel or in fact know are unethical or inappropriate. Below are some of the more common things we tell ourselves to justify what we really know are unjustified actions. As long as we admit what we are doing, basically lying to ourselves, the examples below do not really need much of an explanation.

1. Call It by a Different Name.

It's a lot easier to "smooth over the numbers" than "to cook the books." Remember all those songs you downloaded unto your computer? Somehow we feel better calling it "peer to peer file sharing" than perhaps a harsher but more accurate word, "theft." Whenever you're faced with an ethical choice, ask yourself what words someone who disapproves of your decision would use to describe it. If you're contemplating "smoothing the numbers," remind yourself that the SEC might call that "fraud." Do you think the artist who composed the music you downloaded would cheerfully call it peer to peer file sharing? Probably not. The fact that something sounds nice does not make it nice.

2. If I Don't Do It, Somebody Else Will.

Tom runs a liquor store. A sixteen-year-old comes in with a fake ID, which Tom immediately recognizes as fake. Tom knows it is both illegal and ethically wrong to sell the teenager the liquor, but says to himself, "If I don't sell it to him, someone else will." Often we rationalize an unethical act by telling ourselves that it's going to happen anyway, so why not just do it ourselves? Two points to note: First, this may not be true. If you don't sell him the liquor, maybe in fact, nobody else will either. Second, and most importantly, such a statement denies one of the fundamental things that this course is meant to teach you: ethics is not only about doing the right thing for others; it's also about doing the right thing for yourself.

3. Everybody Does It.

First, whenever you hear that "everyone" does or believes something, it probably is not true. But what if it were true? What if we could show that "everyone" engages in a specific unethical act? Does that justify us in doing the same thing? No, it does not. A true ethical perspective looks to bridge the "is" of life with the "ought" of life. It's alright and necessary to recognize the way things are, but it is not alright to then throw up our hands and do nothing about transforming the way things are into the way things ought to be. As I said earlier, true ethics is not about "them." It is about us.

4. I Am Just Following Orders.

Claiming that one was doing only what one was told to do is a common way of attempting to absolve oneself by shifting blame to another. Historically, the most well known group of people to make this claim were the Nazis at the Nuremburg Trials after World War II. The fact that someone else tells you to do something unethical does not make it ethical for you to do so. In one of the major corporate scandals over the past years, investigators interviewed several members of the accounting department of the subject corporation. It was clear to everyone that the accounting was false and misleading, including clear to the accountants. When asked why they did what they did, they said that they were following orders from their boss. Needless to say no one was very impressed with that answer. I do realize, however, that this can be a hard thing to avoid, especially if you are relatively new at a job. Your older and experienced supervisor tells you to do something that you feel is unethical. You might have even asked him about the ethics of his request. He may have said don't worry about it; he knows what he is doing. It may be very difficult to stand up and say no, you will not comply. Just know that these are the times that test your moral courage, that define who and what you are. No one said it would be easy.

5. Shifting Agency—It's Someone Else's Fault.

Sometimes, people will attempt to shift the blame for their own unethical actions onto someone else, sometimes even blaming the victim of the unethical act. An employee might blame the company for his theft, saying that the company is really at fault for its poor internal controls. Someone who breaks into an unlocked car might blame the owner for leaving it unlocked. There have even been lawsuits against fast food businesses claiming that it is their fault that the person eating the fattening foods served in those establishments, well, got fat. This is akin to the "Devil made me do it" argument. We attempt to shift the blame for our actions unto someone or something else instead of taking responsibility for our own actions. Know well that you are indeed the captain of your own soul. It is a rare case indeed where someone or something else "made you do it", and you really had no choice. It's human nature to avoid blaming ourselves for our own misdeeds. But regardless of that nature, the simple truth is that we are responsible for our choices, and those choices have consequences. To claim otherwise is just another rationalization.

6. I'm Only Human.

This is what I call the surrender rationalization. In most other cases we rationalize the situation to put the appearance of a moral or ethical front on something that we know is immoral or unethical. Not here. Here we are saying that yes, I know this is wrong, but hey, I'm not perfect. Overall I am a good and decent person, but just not this time. I congratulate you on your honesty, but not so much on your ethics. Yes, we all make mistakes. We all do things that we know are not always right. But to say what else do you expect from a mere mortal is not a good answer. At the least, learn from the mistake, and try not to repeat it. Maybe you won't be made a saint tomorrow, but at least you will be making progress.

7. There Is Too Much at Stake.

If you could steal ten dollars, and there was no chance of you being caught, would you do it? Most of you would probably say no. (I said most, not all.) However, if you had the chance to steal one million dollars without the chance of being caught would you do that? For a lot of people, this is not such an easy question. Although they may not engage in relatively small acts of dishonesty, when the stakes are a lot higher, the temptation becomes far greater. As a sales manager you would not intentionally lie to a customer. But when your boss tells you that your job is on the line, and you know that without this sale you may be out of a job, would you then lie to the customer to get the sale and keep your job? This is where the concept of moral courage comes in. It doesn't take any real courage to do the right thing when it doesn't cost you anything. This is not the test of the moral person. Rather, if you really want to know whom, and more importantly what kind of person you really are, the true test comes when doing the right thing comes with a price.

8. Nobody Is Really Hurt.

This has to be one of the greatest lies we tell ourselves. Whenever we act unethically almost always someone else is in fact going to be impacted, hurt by our actions. When I say "almost always" I mean that in terms of other people being hurt. In terms of harm that is done to us there is no "almost" about it. Every time we compromise our integrity, we do harm to the person that we are and the person that we hope to be. From an ethical perspective, there is no such thing as a victimless crime. At the least, we are always a victim of our own unethical behavior.

9. Who Am I to Judge?

In an era of political correctness, many have been told that you never have the right to judge someone. To this I would reply, nonsense. Not only do we have the right to judge in many cases, we have a moral duty to judge. If we take the "never judge" idea out to its logical conclusion, this would mean that we would not make any moral distinction between Adolph Hitler and Mother Theresa. Likewise in our dealings with others, the fact of the matter is that there are some bad people in the world. We can usually identify them by their actions. When we encounter such actions and people, not only can we judge, but also we should judge if for no other reason than to protect us and society from those sorts of people. There are those who may say, "There are no bad people, just bad actions." Perhaps so, but in the everyday real world in which we live, this distinction may lose some of its charm. Although there may be reasons why some people do bad things, that does not justify the evil done. (See Confusing Explanation with Justification" as a logical fallacy above.)

10. I Could Be Worse.

You are considering an unethical action. In trying to justify the decision you say to yourself, "Hey, compared to a lot of other people, I could be doing a lot worse." And this may be true. On a comparative basis of bad acts, it is true that stealing a few company supplies may not rise to the same level of wrongful acts as robbing a bank. However, simply because it is true that you could be a worse person is not a convincing argument as to why you should not be a better person.

11. Just This One Time.

We know that we should not do what we are thinking about doing, and upon reflection we conclude that we have never done anything like this before, and we certainly will never do anything like this again because this is not the type of person that we really are or want to be. However, right now, well, maybe just this once it will be all right. No, it isn't. Every time we take an action, for better or for worse, we are engaged in the process of self-definition. The unfortunate truth of matter is that once we tell that lie or we cheat, even though we have told ourselves we will never do it again because we are not a liar or a cheater, the easier it becomes to lie or cheat again in the future. If we are defining ourselves by our actions, (which, rest assured is how other people will define us) exactly how many lies do we have to tell until we are officially a liar? How many times do we have to cheat on an exam before we are officially a cheater? "Just this one time" rarely turns out to be true.

12. But This Is Business.

I've saved the best to last. This rationalization is used as a justification for all types of actions that most ethical people would never engage in if they were dealing with their own personal affairs. The rationalization is based on a totally false premise: that there is such a thing as "business." There isn't. There are only people: people who own the business, who manage the business, and who work for the business. There may be a lot of people, but there is no one named "Mr. Business." From an ethics perspective, business is nothing more than an activity in which people engage. There is no moral justification for keeping two sets of ethical books. One set of books that you have written as a guide to your personal moral life, and then some other set of books that seems to be different from the first. This second set of books often has very different moral standards than the first and usually much lower standards at that. What is the justification for this second set of lower moral standards? "Well, this is for business." Let's make this easy. There is only one set of books. If you would not act in a particular way in your personal life, there is no justification for acting differently within the context of your business life.

This is only a partial list of the various things we tell ourselves to rationalize otherwise questionable ethical behavior. People can be very creative in coming up with explanations/excuses for their actions. Care to add a few examples of your own?

2.7 CHAPTER HIGHLIGHTS

1. What do we mean by critical thinking?

Critical thinking is reasonable thinking. It is not blind acceptance of any proposition that cannot be supported in reason or by the evidence.

2. Why is critical thinking an important skill?

It "is our only guarantee against delusion, deception, superstition, and misapprehension of ourselves and our earthly circumstances."

3. How is it that we know something to be true, or at least believe something to be true?

One way is through the observation of empirical evidence and another way is because it is logical to do so.

4. What are some of the logical fallacies you are exposed to?

Appeal to False Authority
Red Herring
Attacking the Person
False Dichotomies
Fallacy of Complex Questions
The Gambler's Fallacy
Argument by Threat
Circular Arguments
Reasoning from the Relative to the Absolute
Perception is Reality
Fallacy of Free Choice
Confusing Legality with Morality
Confusing Causation with Correlation
Fallacy of Small Numbers
Confusing Explanation with Justification
Emotional Appeal
False Analogy
Confusing Freedom of Speech/Religion with Truth

5. What are some common rationalizations?

Call it by a different name.
If I don't do it, somebody else will.
Everybody does it.

I am Just Following Orders.

Shifting Agency—It's someone else's fault.

I'm only human.

There's too much at stake.

Nobody is really hurt.

Who am I to judge?

I could be worse.

Just this one time.

But this is business.

PROBLEM FOR DISCUSSION

How far will we go in justifying what we believe to be true? Social Psychologist Leon Festinger in his 1956 book, *When Prophesy Fails*,[1] told the following story about the end of the world.

> In the early 1950s, one Marian Keech claimed that through automatic writing, she had received messages from aliens whom she called the Guardians. They told Keech that God was going to destroy the world by a flood, and she and those who choose to follow her should take cover. She was able to gather up a number of followers who called themselves The Seekers or The Brotherhood of the Seven Rays. Keech told them that the aliens had revealed to her that right before the flood hits, they, the true believers, would be picked up by flying saucers and saved from destruction. Even the date was revealed: December 21, 1954. Her followers left their jobs and families to follow Keech and await the day of salvation. As it turned out, December 21 came and went with neither a flood nor a visit from the flying saucers. Did this present a problem for Keech? No, it did not. She told her followers that she received a telepathic message from the Guardians telling her that God was so pleased with the faith that she and her followers had shown that God had decided to cancel the earth's destruction. Was this then the end of the Seekers? No, not at all. Of the eleven members of her group only two left. The others were more convinced than ever of Keech's abilities. It seems that her failed prophesy, coupled with her explanation, solidified the belief of the remaining members, and the group continued to exist for many years thereafter.

If someone was trying to convince you that you should join this group, what objections, if any, might you raise?

1 Festinger, Leon; Henry W. Riecken, Stanley Schachter (1956). *When Prophecy Fails: A Social and Psychological Study of a Modern Group that Predicted the Destruction of the World.* University of Minnesota Press. ISBN 1-59147-727-1. Reissued 2008 by Pinter & Martin with a foreword by Elliot Aronson, ISBN 978-1-905177-19-6.

CHAPTER THREE

Ethical Theory and Business

3.1 INTRODUCTION

It's a jungle out there. It's probably not a secret to anyone reading this that jobs are hard to get. The better the job, the harder it is. One of, if not the primary reason that most students major in some business discipline is in hopes of getting that good job when they graduate. Although you may be truly special to Mom, Dad, Grandma and Grandpa, you will soon find out that when it comes to the job market, you are only as special as you can factually prove yourself to be. The competition is fierce. So what are you to do? What does it look like a lot of other people are doing? Here's a sample. According to research by The Society of Human Resource Managers, over 53 percent of individuals outright lie on their resume, and some 78 percent of resumes are at least misleading. Here are some of the numbers:

- 78 percent of all resumes are misleading.
- 21 percent state fraudulent degrees.
- 29 percent show altered employment dates.
- 40 percent have inflated salary claims.
- 33 percent have inaccurate job descriptions.

- 27 percent give falsified references.
- 3 percent have a misdemeanor conviction.
- 7 percent have a felony conviction.

What about college students? The numbers aren't any better. According to the same study, when college students were asked if they would lie on their resume to get their ideal job, over 70 percent said they would. Getting to the heart of the matter, would you? Is it really so wrong to do so? What about cheating on an exam? Is that so far removed from lying on a resume?

How you answer these questions is going to be based on what moral principles or personal code of conduct you believe in. This leads to a question that has been debated since time immemorial: how do we decide what is right and wrong? It's an old question with many answers. In this chapter, we are going to look at seven of the most popular and/or compelling answers to this question. Some of them are relatively simple and straightforward, others, maybe not so much. But they're all important because people use them knowingly or not to make decisions that can impact the rest of their lives.

As we go through each of the seven systems, read them with a critical eye. Ask yourself, "Do these ethical systems make sense?" Also, keep your own ways of moral reasoning in mind. Chances are very good that you have adopted parts of these systems into your own way of thinking. This is a good opportunity for self-reflection and self-criticism, which, if you haven't noticed, is a big part of what this course (and college itself), is all about.

3.2 ETHICAL RELATIVISM

Ethical relativism is the belief that there are no objective or absolute truths in ethics. What is morally right or wrong varies from person to person or from society to society. For instance, relativism says that lying, cheating and stealing aren't necessarily wrong for everyone everywhere; they're only wrong in certain cultures and at certain times. Simply put, what's wrong for me isn't necessarily wrong for you depending on the time and the culture. On its face, this may seem reasonable. Every society develops its own standards of behavior defining what is acceptable, and what is not within that society. So it stands to reason that as societies differ from place to place and from historical time-to-time, so are the standards used by those societies. Thus, there are no real absolutes. Only varying standards based on time and place. Not a bad argument. However, let's consider some counter arguments.

First, and going directly to the heart of relativism, is it true that there are no objective or absolute truths? Simply because people may disagree about something does not in itself mean that there is not an objective truth to be found in the matter. James Rachels gives a great example of this, noting that people even disagree about scientific matters. For instance, "some people believe that disease is caused by evil spirits, while others believe it is caused by microbes, but we do not on that account conclude that disease has no "real" cause. The same might be true of ethics—disagreement might only mean that some people are more enlightened than others."[1]

More so, at least from the perspective of ethics, there may be a lot more cross-cultural agreement than we at first realize. For example, it is difficult to find cultures that think murder is a great thing, or that snatching an elderly woman's purse is something to proudly write home to Mom about. From even a business perspective, you would be hard pressed to find any culture that thought dishonesty and not honoring your contracts was a fundamentally good thing. No, in order for any society, at any time to exist and survive, there seems to be some, (we can debate how many), ethical principles that are universally deemed true. The judgments used in applying those principles may vary from place to place and from time to time, but the principles themselves seem immutable.

This leads us to the next objection to relativism. If we were to accept that there are no moral absolutes, then we lose the ability to criticize even the most outrageous of practices that we may encounter in a given society at a given time. For example, if we encounter a society that is engaging in genocide, is it proper for us to say that this is objectively wrong? Or do we have to look up and say well, that's what that particular society believes is the right thing to do, so we can't criticize?

But wait. If we say that there may be objective moral truth, doesn't that lead us to intolerance of other people's cultures and beliefs? (And as we all know, intolerance is something that we can never tolerate.) Yes, it can and does. This is not to say that we shouldn't exercise a great deal of caution and work very hard to understand the other person's point of view. We should. But at the end of the day, there is nothing wrong with condemning those parts of the nineteenth century American South that defended slavery, nor the anti-Semitic aspects of certain segments of German society in the early twentieth century. How about the practice of female genital mutilation practiced in some cultures today? And what of our own society? Is it right for us to condemn cases of racial discrimination? Or do we say only that if a part of our society believes that discrimination is morally acceptable, then we cannot criticize? It is suggested that not only can we be morally intolerant of these practices and beliefs, we should be.

Finally, this brings us full circle back to critical thinking. Ethical relativism can be a conversation-stopper. All a person has to say is "It's part of my culture," and the conversation's over. There is no critical reflection regarding the morality of the position at issue. Oftentimes it is nothing more than saying, "That's just what I (or they) were taught" or "That's just what I believe."

3.3 EGOISTIC ETHICS

Egoistic ethics is a me-first philosophy. It claims that a person should always act to advance his or her own interests. A person should not be concerned with the needs, desires or rights of others except inasmuch as such concern results in self-benefit. Going back to our opening question regarding lying on a resume, for the egoist this

---

1 "ethical relativism." *Encyclopædia Britannica. Encyclopædia Britannica Online Academic Edition.* Encyclopædia Britannica Inc., 2012. Web. 25 Jun. 2012. <http://www.britannica.com/EBchecked/topic/194016/ethical-relativism>.

is not a difficult question. If it appears to be in his or her best interest to do so, then go ahead and lie.

Like many other ethical systems, egoistic ethics' greatest strength, advancing one's own interests, is also its greatest weakness. Certainly a system that places the self as effectively the center of the ethical universe can be very attractive to people. But let's consider the downside. Concepts of duty or loyalty, be it to others or society, are of greatly diminished value. The same may be true for any other perceived virtue that involves anyone or anything outside of us. Is love or friendship truly attainable for an egoist? More so, it is not difficult to come up with examples of a given person's wants and desires that most of us would consider immoral. Some argue that "egoistic ethics" is almost a contradiction in terms. Can we really talk about a system of ethics that by and large only concerns itself with the individual and places little to no value on others except in so far as those others can benefit the individual? Does this qualify as an ethic at all?

3.4 KANTIAN (DEONTOLOGICAL) ETHICS

Welcome to the world of eighteenth century philosopher Immanuel Kant. The bad news is that he is one of the more difficult philosophers that we will encounter. The good news is that for our purposes, we can summarize the key elements of his theory without too much pain. So follow along.

One of the foundational distinctions underlying all of Kant's philosophy is that of the situational and universal. Kantian ethics draws on this distinction by providing universal principles that can be applied in any given situation. Kant calls these universal principles "categorical imperatives." By "categorical" Kant means that they apply in all situations without exception. By "imperative" he means that it is always a person's duty to obey them, which is how we get the phrase "deontological ethics," which simply means "duty ethics." Kant claims that the categorical imperatives are universal because they may be determined through pure reason alone. As such, they can be known by anyone who has the ability to reason. Simply put, it is imperative to act ethically for the simple reason that it is reasonable to do so.

So using his pure reason, Kant came up with the categorical imperatives. Kant formulates the first in this way, "Act only according to that maxim whereby you can at the same time will that it should become a universal law without contradiction."[2] This means that we should only do something if we think that all people everywhere should also do it. For example, when faced with the choice of whether or not to lie, we should choose not to lie, because it is unreasonable for a person to desire all people everywhere to lie in every situation. That would be chaos.

Kant formulates the second categorical imperative in this way, "Act in such a way that you treat humanity, whether in your own person or in the person of any other, never merely as a means to an end, but always at the same time as an end."[3] The meaning

---

2 Kant, Immanuel; translated by James W. Ellington [1785] (1993). *Grounding for the Metaphysics of Morals 3rd ed.* Hackett. pp. 30.
3 Ibid.

of Kant's second categorical imperative is much more apparent than the first: human beings are ends in themselves, never means to other ends. No person should ever use anyone, including oneself, as only a means to achieve some other end.

It is perhaps important to point out what Kant is *not* saying in his second categorical imperative. Kant is not saying that one should never use or employ a person in order to achieve an end. For Kant, it is perfectly acceptable to hire a factory worker as a means to producing a good, but the worker must be treated and viewed as more than just that means. People may be viewed or treated as ends and means at the same time, but never treated only as a means. This requires that no matter what the transaction or relationship is between two persons, they must always treat each other with mutual respect.

Kant offers a compelling ethical system because it is highly objective and because it offers clear means for navigating ethical dilemmas: here's the rule. Now follow it. However, it is susceptible to a few major criticisms.

First, Kant claims that our only motivation to be ethical should be because it is rational to do so. In effect, this means that the parents who endure hardship for their children on the basis of a cold, detached rationality are acting more ethically than the parents who do the same out of love for their children. For Kant, we should not give to charity or visit the sick for the pleasure involved in improving another person's quality of life; we should do so only out of a disinterested obedience to duty. Thus, Kantian ethics' greatest strength may also be its greatest weakness: unwavering rationality. We might say that Kantian ethics are so resolutely rational that they wrongfully ignore the ethical dimensions of that other human faculty: emotion.

Second, Kantian ethics dictate that the consequences of our actions have no bearing on their moral standing even if the consequences are well known before we ever act. Try this. A friend knocks on your door telling you some evil people are looking to kill him. You hide him in your basement. The evil people knock on your door and ask you if you know where your friend is. Do you lie or say, yes, down in the basement, second door on the right. Kantian ethics would require that you tell the truth. Lying is, after all, a violation of the first categorical imperative, because we cannot rationally wish that everyone in all places and at all times lie. Thus, Kant would claim, the ethical thing to do in such a situation is to tell the truth, even if it leads to the loss of totally innocent life. Needless to say, in certain situations, that's a difficult position to accept.

A third criticism of Kant is that not everyone may agree on the rules, even using pure reason. The idea of course is that different people using their reason may come to different conclusions as to what a universal rule might be. As we talked about with relativism, there may be some absolutes that it appears everyone may agree upon, but how many and what are they? In fairness to Kant, he might answer that there are more than you may think. Ask yourself what are things that you would never want anyone to do to you, ever, under any circumstances. That may be a fairly long list. Therefore, Kant might conclude, presuming you are rational, those should be universal to all.

3.5 UTILITARIAN ETHICS

Whereas Kantian ethics has little regard for the consequences of a moral action, utilitarian ethics maintains just the opposite. The only thing that the utilitarian cares about is consequences. For a utilitarian, an action is just if it "produces at least as much good (utility) for all people affected by the action as any alternative action."[4] Another more simple and common way of putting this is that an action is just if it results in the greatest good for the greatest number of people.

Utilitarian ethics has practical purpose as one of its greatest strengths, at least insofar as it is goal-oriented. It is far more inclined to look at how things are as opposed to how things ought to be. In making any moral decision, the utilitarian will generally only ask what are the real and practical consequences of our choices. On its face, utilitarianism seems very attractive. However, before we jump to embrace this philosophy, it's important to understand its deficiencies.

To begin, this theory is based on maximizing the "greatest good". This obviously raises the question, what exactly is that "good" that we are trying to maximize? Whereas one person might claim that love is the greatest good, another might claim happiness, justice, loyalty, dignity, life or any other number of things.

For the sake of exploring utilitarianism, let's temporarily assume that philosophers have settled such arguments, and, as Aristotle concluded, there is only one value worth increasing: happiness. Now remember that utilitarianism is comparative by nature—sort of a balance sheet concept. It assesses the moral content of an action by comparing its effects on a value, happiness in our case, to that of all other plausible alternatives. So now the question is, does Action X increase or decrease the overall level of happiness in the world? As you might guess, the problems with quantifying and predicting the effects of an action on an individual's happiness (much less that of a multitude of individuals) are many.

First, how, or more frighteningly, who determines what the "greatest good" is? Who specifically is to decide what is the greatest good for the greatest many? Do we take a vote? What of individual integrity? Finally, what of the problem of unforeseen consequences? We may not know if our decision today for the greatest good turns out to be right until sometime in the future, and maybe far into the future. What if we were wrong? Can we really know all who will be affected by our decision, for better or for worse? Such questions have no apparent and workable answers.

Second, as there is no "ordering" or priority of benefits, the system does not deal with conflicts very well. Deciding between competing "goods" can be a problem. For example, it is a good that people have health care. It is also a good that business creates value for its shareholders. What happens if these two "goods" come into conflict, such as in cases of pre-existing conditions? What's good for the insurance business and its shareholders, not insuring people with pre-existing conditions, is obviously not so good for those having those conditions. This is not to mention the obvious problem that a perceived good by one person or group may be very subjective and be quite different from a perceived good for another person or group.

---

4 Cambridge Dictionary of Philosophy, 943-944

Third, the system ignores "non-utilitarian issues" such as justice and individual rights, which by definition can't be weighed on a scale or compared on a balance sheet. In the 1970s, Pol Pot was the leader of Cambodia. In his desire to create the "perfect state", he executed upwards of two million people, including those over 65 years of age and those with physical handicaps. As a pure utilitarian play, he believed that these people did not contribute to the betterment of society. They were, if you will, a net liability on his balance sheet for achieving state happiness. Their very existence resulted in a "disutility" that he was determined to fix. And what of our own terminally ill patients in hospitals today? Some may argue that it may be in society's crude "best interest" to deny health benefits to these people as this is a "waste of resources." Should we start "pulling plugs" on all of them? Can a utilitarian really conceive of a situation where an individual's right to something (like life) can have a value greater than the needs of society at any given time and place? Hopefully you see the problem.

If we drop the assumption that happiness is the only value, and admit to other values such as justice, the problems associated with utilitarianism multiply. What of actions that result in an increase in the world's level of happiness but a decrease in the world's level of justice? It is not difficult to imagine that robbing the five thousand wealthiest people in the world and using their wealth to feed, clothe and provide medicine for millions could result in more happiness for more people, but does that justify robbing five thousand people? Because utilitarianism seemingly cannot provide a single intrinsic value, or prioritize between multiple intrinsic values, it cannot provide any clear direction for dealing with situations in which an increase in one value results in a decrease in another. Utilitarianism's goal, creating a world of greater value, may be admirable, but it may fail to provide any guidance on what that value might be or how to measure it.

3.6 DEISTIC ETHICS

Deistic Ethics, or Divine Command Theory, refers to an ethical system in which a God or group of gods tell us what is right and what is wrong.

One advantage of a deistic ethics system is its perceived clarity. We know what is right and wrong because we are told what is right and wrong from an infallible source. And as long as we are dealing with a homogeneous group, this may work well within that given group or society. In a diverse society, this system obviously becomes a bit more problematic. Simply stated, which god or gods does a particular person believe in? Moreover, various religious beliefs may take various and differing moral positions, which, in extreme cases can lead to societal strife. Last, interpretations of divine commands can vary wildly even within the same belief structure.

3.7 THE ETHICS OF CARE

The Ethics of Care emphasizes the importance of human relationships in making ethical choices. In doing so, it pays special attention to the fact that we all depend on one another to achieve our own goals. Furthermore, it emphasizes the need to pay special attention to those who might be particularly vulnerable to the consequences of our actions.

We could contrast this system with Kantian ethics. Kant wants to find universal principles that apply to all situations. Once he has those principles, he's not interested at all in the situation itself. Kant doesn't care about the context of an ethical choice, or the people involved; in fact, avoiding basing decisions on those factors is the whole point of Kantian ethics. The ethics of care, on the other hand, makes context and people supreme. Who's affected? How? What is my relationship to them? Do I have a special responsibility to them? Are they strong or weak? According to the ethics of care, the answers to these questions should provide the basis for our decisions.

This system allows for nuance in a way that most ethical systems do not. Utilitarians care about consequences, but they do not prioritize relationships to family, friends or societies. Utilitarians are fine with making a miserable person slightly more miserable while making a happy person moderately happier, as long as the overall level of happiness in the world increases. The ethics of care takes more into account. It may include other perceived virtues or factors such as compassion and human emotion as part of the decision making process. In doing so it presents a more "human-centered" approach than perhaps some other theories. As you've heard before, this strength is also a weakness. In allowing for so many nuances and emphasizing the importance of relationships, the ethics of care makes it difficult to resolve competing ethical claims because we have different relationships that might give us varying amounts of responsibility to others. The ethics of care can make things so complicated that it becomes difficult to understand what our responsibility truly is in any given situation.

3.8 VIRTUE ETHICS

We might say that Kantian ethics wants to create good actions based on moral duty, that utilitarian ethics wants to create good consequences and a better world and that the ethics of care wants to highlight the importance of human relationships in ethical decision-making. When it comes to virtue ethics, we might say that it wants to create better people.

The virtue ethicist identifies certain virtues, or positive traits, that a person should cultivate. Having these virtues is what makes a person good, and not having them is what makes a person bad. You might ask, "What about our actions? Aren't virtue ethicists concerned with those?" Of course they are, but indirectly, because once you make good people, you don't really have to worry about telling them to do the good thing or even what the good thing is. Virtuous people know what's good and do it simply because that's the kind of people they are. Virtue ethics starts at the source of actions (and therefore the source of consequences): the individual. In this way, virtue ethicists get to have their cake and eat it too. It works like this. If you make good people, they will make good decisions, and when all goes well, good decisions will lead to good consequences.

You might be thinking, that's all well and good, but how do we become or make virtuous people, or even know what virtue is? A virtue ethicist might answer that you are probably over thinking this. You probably already know the answer. Think of some people you know whom you consider good and some people you know whom you consider bad. At first, it might be tough to identify what exactly makes them good or bad, but it doesn't usually take too long to start putting the picture together. This person is good because she's honest, hard-working, cares about her family and just somehow tends to do the "right" thing more often than not. That person is bad because she's underhanded, and a lazy mooch who doesn't seem to care much about others, and she just seems to do the "bad" thing more often than not. Most, if not all of us already have a sense of what's right and what's wrong. The virtue ethicist wants you to work on developing and obeying that sense.

How do you go about that? Easy: practice. Think of that good person you know, and when you go throughout your day, ask yourself, what would he do? Then do it. It's that simple. Over time, you'll become more like that person, until you're doing the right thing more often and having to think about it less. The goal is for the right thing to become the natural thing; doing good should be automatic. When that happens, you've become a virtuous person. The beauty of virtue ethics lies in its simplicity and in its ability to create not just good people, but also good actions and, hopefully, good consequences.

Virtue ethics does have some problems. Sometimes we might know two virtuous people who disagree on what the right thing to do in a certain situation might be; this makes imitating the good person difficult. There's no easy solution to this problem, and in fact, there really might not be a "right" thing to do at all (remember those ethical dilemmas)? Perhaps the best response is that as long as we're all trying our best to be like one of two virtuous people, things are probably going to be better for it.

Perhaps the greatest criticism of virtue ethics consists in the question, "What counts as a virtue?" After all, the entire goal of virtue ethics is to cultivate virtues and thereby create virtuous people. Virtue ethicists disagree on the answer to this question. Aristotle, who, along with Plato, was one of the first virtue ethicists, lists nine virtues: wisdom, prudence, justice, fortitude, courage, liberality, magnificence, magnanimity and temperance. The critic might ask, "Is he right? No more than nine and no less? Cultivate these nine things, and you're all of a sudden a virtuous person?" Obviously not. The virtue ethicist might respond that ethics isn't about making lists of rights and wrongs or good traits and bad; *it's more human* than that, and we shouldn't get too hung up on the details. Ethics is about making good people. Given the flexibility of language, we could probably describe a virtuous person with fewer than nine words, and we could certainly describe them with more. The point is that quibbling over the tiny details of this virtue or that misses the point of ethics entirely. We can learn what good and bad are, however we might try to describe them, from other people, and we can learn to do good and bad from other people as well. And with enough practice, we'll end up either good or bad ourselves.

3.9 CHAPTER HIGHLIGHTS

1. What is Ethical Relativism?

Ethical relativism is the belief that right and wrong vary from one place and time to another.

2. What is Ethical Egoism?

Ethical Egoism is the belief that right and wrong have nothing to do with anything except one's own interests. If it makes me better off, then it's right. If it makes me worse off, then it's wrong.

3. What is Kantian Ethics?

Kantian ethics offers universal principles (categorical imperatives) that can be applied in every situation. The two most important of such principles are the following: Only do something if you can reasonably think that all people everywhere should always do it, and always treat people as ends in themselves, never as only a means.

4. What is Utilitarian Ethics?

Utilitarian Ethics says that something is good as long as it increases the overall amount of value in the world. "The greatest good for the greatest number" is its motto.

5. What is Deistic Ethics?

Deistic Ethics says that right and wrong are revealed to us by God or Gods.

6. What is the Ethics of Care?

The Ethics of Care says that we should consider our relationships with others as well as those affected by our actions, especially the vulnerable, whenever we make ethical decisions.

7. What is Virtue Ethics?

Virtue Ethics wants to create good people. It says that we should practice doing things, and that eventually, we will start doing them automatically.

PROBLEM FOR DISCUSSION

Thousands of years ago there was a once-prosperous kingdom that had fallen into poverty because of a prolonged drought. The king had been very prudent in the years leading up to the drought, saving grain and other foodstuffs for whenever such a change of fortune would arrive. Despite the king's prudence, when the drought finally came it lasted much longer than anyone could have reasonably foreseen.

When the kingdom had only a few months of food left, envoys from another kingdom arrived with an offer. In exchange for unlimited supplies of food and water, the king could sell 20 percent of the population into slavery. The selection of the slaves would be by lottery. As such, even the king and his family could be taken. The civilization making the offer had a reputation for dire treatment of slaves, and the king knew that those sold would be so utterly miserable, malnourished and mistreated that death by starvation would be far preferable to life in slavery.

The king had to make a choice. He could sacrifice 20 percent of the population to save the rest. Or he could hope for the drought to lift in the very near future, knowing that in all likelihood every last man, woman and child, including himself, would slowly and painfully starve to death.[1]

Which choice should the king make? How would the ethical systems we presented earlier answer the question, and how would they get to their answers? What do you think the king should do? Why?

---

1 This case was created by William Ricketts

CHAPTER FOUR

The Decision Making Process

4.1 INTRODUCTION

We all make bad decisions. Fortunately, most of the time, we live to tell the story. If you want to have some fun with your friends, try sitting around and sharing with each other some of the dumbest things that you have ever done. Presuming that there is some honesty in this discussion, a few things will become clear. First, no matter how bad of a mistake you think you have made, someone else has made the same one, and maybe even worse. Second, no one of us has actually committed an original sin. Whatever it was that we did, someone else has already done the same thing, and again, probably worse. As such, it's probably not a good use of your time to continue to beat yourself up over a bad decision. Instead, if your friends are telling the truth, you can look for the common threads that are always present in how we came to make that bad decision. Once we identify those threads, our job is to try as best we can to learn from the mistake and try not to do it again.

In this chapter, we are going to first look at the factors that go in to making a good ethical decision. Then we will discuss why we sometimes do the wrong thing, even when we know it's wrong. In considering the decision making process be sure to remember your critical thinking skills and see how you might be applying the particular ethical theory or theories that you live by.

4.2 THE PROCESS

As the title of this chapter implies, making an ethical decision is a process. Sometimes the process is quick and easy and requires very little thought on our part. It's Friday afternoon. The TV is broken, and you're bored. A friend says to you, "Hey, want to go out and rob a gas station?" For most of us, at least it is hoped, this is not a decision that requires a great deal of thought on our part. (Hint: the answer is no.) Unfortunately, many of the decisions that we are called upon to make, and this is especially true in business, are not that quick and easy to respond to. Remember the sweatshop question that we proposed in Chapter One? When we confront legitimate ethical dilemmas, our decision-making ability will be tested to its extreme. So how should we approach these situations? Step by step. But a word of caution here. The following five steps may seem a bit mechanical. In practice, nothing is ever quite that simple. These steps may flow into each other, but not always in the order that we might hope. So with that said, let's take a look at the process.

Step One: First, determine the objective facts. This is a lot easier said than done. Figuring out the who, what, when and where of a given circumstance can be a tricky business. As we said earlier, facts have a nasty habit of changing, especially as more information is received. To complicate matters further, there may often be a time constraint. We simply may not have all day to make a decision. So what do we do? As a general rule, you do the best you can with the facts that you have when you have them. Does this mean that you may be basing a decision on imperfect or in some situations, straight out wrong information? Yes it does, and get used to that. More often than not we don't have all of the facts when the time comes to a make a decision. So first identify the facts that you do have, at least as well as you understand them to be.

If you are in a group environment trying to reach an ethical consensus with your co-workers, avoid what we call a "stipulation error". That is, where someone says, well, at least we can all agree that X is true. Before you hurry to give your consent, be sure that you in fact do agree that X is true, based on whatever facts may exist. Likewise, watch out for definitions. We may have a set of facts that demonstrates that Jones is dead, and that Green caused his death. Does that fact lead us to reasonably conclude that Green murdered Jones? No, it does not. There has been a killing, the taking of another's life. We can stipulate to that. However, murder is generally defined as the unjust taking of another person's life. Do the facts as we have them lead us to that conclusion? No. Perhaps the killing was justified and thus not murder.

Finally, remember in Chapter Two where we discussed logical fallacies? When it comes to facts, one of the more difficult fallacies to deal with in the decision making process is confusing perception with reality. Most of the "facts" that we claim to know from empirical evidence are based on our perceptions of that evidence. We feel that a flame is hot and conclude that as a general proposition, all flames are hot. But remember Galileo? Many simply looked up and saw that it appeared that the sun revolved around the earth. Seeing is believing, right? But they were wrong. Thus is the nature of facts. Try as we might, we can, and will get them wrong. However, a reasoned decision must always start with some fact or facts, at least as we believe them to be. That is why this is always our starting point. Just don't be shocked if sometimes we get it wrong.

Step Two: Identify as much as possible exactly what the ethical problem or dilemma may be. In other words, what is it here that is bothering you? Is it a legal issue? A professional or corporate issue? Is it something that is client based? Is there a problem with industry standards? Is there a regulatory conflict? Are we looking at a problem with a combination of any of these? Or on even a higher level, is there a particular moral principle that you feel is in jeopardy of being violated? Sometimes we may just have a bad feeling about something. The situation in question fails to pass the "sniff test." That is to say, "I don't know exactly what is going on here, but something doesn't smell right." Although this doesn't sound very scientific, never underestimate the sniff test. Experience seems to tells us that when something really doesn't' "smell right" that's probably because something isn't right. However, upon reflection, sometimes whatever it is that is bothering you may not be anything more than just that, a bad feeling. For example, we may think that our actions may violate a legal or regulatory rule. However, upon looking at it more closely, and perhaps speaking to others such as our lawyer, we may find there is no issue at all. But to do that, we obviously must first identify the potential concern.

Step Three: Identify all of those who may be affected by the issue and the decisions that you make regarding the issue. It is a rare ethical situation indeed that affects no one but us. We are not islands. What we do or fail to do can have profound effects on many others and this is especially true in business. We often refer to these others as stakeholders. A stakeholder can be broadly defined to mean anyone who has an interest in the outcome or actions of our business. Primary stakeholders would be shareholders, managers, employees, suppliers, customers and the local community. We refer to these as "primary" because generally, the lack of any one of these would have a direct and negative impact on the business. We could also consider so-called secondary stakeholders. These would include anyone else that may claim to be affected by, or have an interest in the business, but without whom the business can by and large function without. These might include competitors, special interest groups and the like. You can use this as a sort of checklist in the decision making process. Who is effected by the issue in question? Go down the list of stakeholders (usually focusing on the primary stakeholders) and ask in each instance, how they would respond to the problem. You may conclude that in each case, the effects on and responses of the stakeholders may be positive, negative, or mixed.

Remember our discussion of the pharmaceutical company in Chapter One? This was the case where your company was the sole manufacturer of a drug that could cure a fatal disease common in Africa. The only problem was that the people who needed it the most did not have the ability to pay for it. So what do you do? If you decide to give it away, who is affected by this decision? The patients in Africa are affected most certainly, and presumably for the better. However, are there other stakeholders who may experience a different outcome? Yes. What about the shareholders, the owners of the company? Giving the drug away would decrease the company's profits, and thereby negatively impact the owners. What about suppliers, especially those who supply capital to the company such as banks and other lenders? Would they be negatively impacted by this decision? Other suppliers may take a positive view as now you have to buy more supplies from these venders. And if profits go down? Does that mean that perhaps the company may not need so many employees and managers? Maybe. How would the local community be effected? And what of your other customers? Might they feel that they are paying an inflated price for your product to support the give-away to the customers in Africa? How might they respond? And if you decide not to give it away? Certainly the impact on the patients is catastrophic. Could this result in bad publicity for the company, which in turn could also hurt profits? Perhaps. The point we are making is that regardless of your decision, it has effects that reach many people, so make your decisions carefully.

Also bear in mind that harmful effects may be more than just economic effects on you and your company. Your company may be considering relocating its facility to another state. Usually the reason given for this action is that it will save the company money. However, remember our stakeholders. How would this decision affect the employees of the company? Are they to be laid off? What of their families? How about the local community that has depended on your company to provide everything from a tax base to the town to other businesses in the vicinity that depend on the company for their survival? The local restaurants, movie theatres and even schools may face significant harm from your decision. Ethical decision-making requires that we consider all who are affected by our actions.

Step Four: What are our options? We know what the problem is. We have identified all the parties that may be affected by the situation, or at least we think we have. Now it's time to figure out what to do about the problem. This is the brainstorming part of the process. It is recommended that storming one's brain be considered a group activity, not an individual sport. Other people may bring a perspective and an expertise to the situation that we alone may not have. Sometimes this is an easy call. If we have determined that there may be a legal problem, it probably makes sense to bring in a lawyer. Is it a professional problem? Perhaps our profession has a code of ethics that we can consult for guidance. The point is that there may be alternatives to dealing with the problem that we alone may see. But this is just the beginning of this step.

This step really flows from step three above. Say that we assemble the best minds on our management team to consider alternatives or choices of action to deal with the problem. Each proposed alternative may have its own separate impact on the various stakeholders that we just discussed. As such, we still will want to go down our checklist of effected stakeholders with each proposed alternative choice of action. More so, how we evaluate the different options presented may in very large part depend upon what ethical system in life we have adopted. For example, if you are a utilitarian, you might look up and say alright, we have to weigh all of the advantages against the disadvantages for all of the stakeholders involved. If it appears that more stakeholders are better off with option A than are harmed, then that's what we go with. On the other hand, if you are a follower of virtue ethics you might conclude that despite the fact that this action helps more than harms, it's not something that a virtuous person would do. As for the egoists in the audience, you might conclude that you really do not care how the decision impacts the other stakeholders, all that matters is how the decision impacts you.

Right about now, things may seem to be getting a bit complicated. As a practical matter, how do you really evaluate each of your options while taking into account all the stakeholders who may be affected? Bearing in mind that no system is perfect, where the impacts are not obvious I suggest you consider the following factors in your decision making process.

1. Identify the various harms that each alternative may cause to each stakeholder. You may identify a harm that is so great as to make that alternative unacceptable on its face.

2. Consider the legality of the proposed suggestion. If it is illegal, it's probably not a good idea. It should be added, however, that this might not always be true. As mentioned earlier, there can be situations where violating the law may in fact be the ethical thing to do. Therefore, before you come to this conclusion, you have to be prepared to suffer the legal consequences.

3. What are the practical consequences of any proposed solution? For example, someone may come up with a great suggestion, but administratively, it may be impossible to do. Your company may not have the resources to follow the suggestion, or you do not have the time to implement the proposal. Further, always consider the logical consequences of a decision. Remember that there are two types of consequences. The first are those that are reasonably foreseeable. The second involves the so-called rule of unintended consequences. This is a sort of Murphy's Law of decision making. (Murphy's Law: whatever can go wrong will go wrong.) This "rule" says that try as you may, there are always some unforeseen and unforeseeable consequences to our actions.

4. Consider the public relations effects. If you go with a proposed suggestion, are you prepared to have that published in tomorrow's newspaper? If not, maybe something is wrong.

5. Can you defend the decision? Remember our critical thinking discussions. Can you clearly and logically explain your decision without rationalizing? If not, perhaps this decision should be reexamined.

6. Does your decision pass the "Mom test?" Simply put, what would your Mom say if you told her that this is what you are going to do? Of course Mom might be wrong, and maybe she does not understand all of the intricacies involved in a particular business transaction, but nevertheless, don't underrate her intuition.

7. How does this decision make you feel? As we should not underrate Mom's intuition, we also should not underrate our own intuition. Remember the sniff test? If it really feels wrong to us, there is probably a good reason for that. Your conscience may be telling you something.

8. Does this decision pass the Golden Rule test? In other words, if we were on the receiving end of the decision, how would we react? Is this something that we would want others to do to us? If not, maybe we should reconsider our actions.

9. Does the suggestion or decision pass the business vision test? By this I mean is the proposed action consistent with the values that you and your company espouse? Is this really what you want your company (or yourself) to be known for? If not, you probably should not do it.

Again, the above are factors to be considered. Any one of them may or may not solve the problem in itself. However, if you follow this process, you are in a better position to make the best and most morally informed decision you can.

Step Five: Make a decision. As future business managers this is what you are going to be paid for. As the stakes become greater, and the decisions you make impact more people, know that you will be asked to explain your decisions. If you can show that you followed the process that I have outlined above, you can feel fairly confident that you have done the best you could at the time with the information you had to work with. No one can ask for anything more.

So now we have it, and we are done with the decision making process. Well, not quite. Whenever and if you have the chance, reexamine your decision. Even though you have done everything right as far as following the decision making process, as we talked about in cases of ethical dilemmas, there seldom is a perfect answer. Try as we might, we may find sometimes that the decision we made turned out to have unfortunate consequences that we had not foreseen. Sometimes we have to live with that. Other times, however, we may be able to go back and remedy any mistakes that were made. Do not be afraid to do so. It is not a sign of weakness to say that you were wrong. It is a sign of leadership to say you made a mistake, and here's how you are going to fix it. In either case, we can always learn from our experience so the next time we deal with the same or similar problem we are better prepared to do so.

4.3 WHY WE DO THE WRONG THING

It comes as no surprise that some people do bad things. The question is why? Psychologists, criminologists and a raft of other "ists" have been struggling with this question for millennia, and we do not intend to solve that question here. However, from the standpoint of business ethics, there are certain traits and circumstances that seem to repeat themselves regularly when it comes to unethical decision making. For the rest of this chapter, we are going to take a look at some of those traits and circumstances to better understand and recognize them when we see them in our business lives.

4.4 A QUESTION OF VALUES

As was just said, some people do bad things. On one level this may boil down to a question of values. If we value something, we will take steps to achieve or preserve that value. For instance, if we say that honesty is a value, then we will conduct ourselves in such a way as to be honest. If we do not consider honesty as a value, then we have no problem with lying and the like. So what do we value? What are the things in life, especially character traits, that we consider valuable? If you have never asked yourself this question before, now is as good a time as any. Take a few moments out now and write down the values or virtues that you consider important to you. Don't try to list them in any particular order. Just decide what you consider to be important in defining who you are, or the person whom you would like to be. The following is a short list of some of the virtues that society over the centuries has considered valuable. You may or may not agree, but here is a starting point for your personal list. You may think of others.

Caring	Compassion	Courage
Courtesy	Forgiveness	Generosity
Honesty	Honor	Humility
Integrity	Justice	Kindness
Loyalty	Moderation	Modesty
Patience	Perseverance	Reliability
Self-discipline	Trustworthiness	Tolerance

So how does your list look? You chose all of them? Added a few others? That's fine. Now, from your list, pick three. Write them down. Commit them to memory. For the rest of your life, remember that today, this date, you determined that these are the virtues that you most value; that when other people think of you, at the very least, these are the qualities for which you will be known and remembered for.

Now comes the hard part. You have identified those values or virtues that you consider to be most important in your life. The next question is: how important are they? For example, most people would consider honesty as one of their key virtues. Very few want to be known as a liar. With that being said, remember our question in Chapter Three regarding lying on your resume? Some 70 percent of college students admitted that they would do so if it helped them get their ideal job. Plus, it's a safe bet that a large portion of that 70 percent would also have said that they consider honesty to be very important, and yet they would lie. Why?

4.5 THE FRAUD TRIANGLE

So why do otherwise good people do bad things? Although there are true villains, most of the time fraud and dishonesty are committed by people who otherwise would never have been suspected of doing anything dishonest. So why do they? The criminologist Donald R. Cressey says there are three factors that must be present for an ordinary person to commit fraud: motivation, rationalization, and opportunity. Cressey calls these the Fraud Triangle. Let's take a look.

Motivation

This can be best understood by simply asking "Why did you do it?" Again, outside of the case of the thoroughly dishonest individual, ordinary people engage in dishonest acts for a reason. They have some incentive to do so. In the vast majority of cases, the old adage, "follow the money and find the truth" applies. Thomas Kaiser offers a good explanation of the process[1] which, with some elaboration of our own, is laid out below.

We can divide motivation for dishonesty into four main categories: financial, vices, work related and other pressures. Let's look at each one individually.

Financial Pressures

Financial pressures typically involve greed, living beyond one's means, high bills or personal debt, poor credit, unexpected financial needs and personal financial losses. Financial pressures can sometimes occur without warning (casualty loss), suddenly (due to vices) or be long-term (disability or sickness). We do not always have control over the varied financial pressures that we experience in life. But regardless of whether the financial need is self-inflicted or caused through no fault of our own, the perceived need for money is the single greatest motivator towards dishonesty.

Vice Pressures

Vice pressures are created due to vices like gambling, drugs/alcohol or extramarital affairs. Simply put, vices are the worst kind of pressure to commit fraud. Anyone who is willing to go through anything to place that bet, get high or find that thrill from an illicit relationship will definitely look for ways to steal from their employer or commit other types of fraud.

Work-Related Pressures

The majority of fraud is motivated by financial or vice pressures. However, in some cases some people will commit fraud to get even with their employer or other people. Some work related pressures might come from getting little recognition for job performance, job dissatisfaction, fear of losing a job, or feeling underpaid.

Other Pressures

Finally, other pressures motivate many fraudsters. They might have a spouse who demands a higher standard of living. Maybe they want a nicer car or a bigger house than their brother-in-law. It is easy to confuse success with net worth. Don't fall into such traps; lasting relationships bring more fulfillment than nice cars or big houses. Remember that life is not all about you, and learn to measure success in other ways than relying on dollars or material possessions.

Rationalizations

We have already spent a lot of time on this in Chapter Two. Suffice it to say that it is very easy to rationalize doing a dishonest deed when you are under significant pressure, be it financial, vice, work-related or other. The good thing about this is that if

---

1 http://ezinearticles.com/7009803 expert=Thomas_R_Kaiser, Cressey's Fraud Triangle - Part 1: Perceived Pressure

you recall our discussion in Chapter Two, you generally know full well when you are rationalizing. When you find yourself in this situation, try to remove the rationalization and call the action what it is. Instead of saying "This is payback to my employer for treating me poorly," say to yourself, "I am going to steal money from my employer." At least then you are being honest with yourself regarding your dishonesty.

Opportunity

People may be tempted to act dishonestly, but without the opportunity to do so, the plan never gets past the thinking stage. This is perhaps more of a management issue in terms of taking steps, through good internal company control and the like, to limit the opportunity for wrongdoing. From the individual perspective, however, opportunity usually involves a two-step process. First, do you have the actual ability to commit the wrongful act? This is a yes or no type of question. If the answer is yes, people in this situation usually then ask the second question. If I do this, what are the odds of getting caught? If we go back to the Kohlberg discussion that we had in Chapter One, we know that a percentage of people operate on the "obedience and punishment" stage of development, and never progress any further. For those, the only reason not to do something wrong is fear of punishment. (For those here at this stage of moral development, as to getting caught, I suggest that the country is full of prisons with people who believed that at the time of the crime that they would not be caught.) Regardless, where there is the ability to commit the wrongful act and little fear of punishment, the third leg of the triangle, opportunity, is complete.

It is when all three of these elements come together, motivation, rationalization and opportunity that usually good people do bad things. We may not always be able to control the circumstances in our lives that give rise to a motivation to be dishonest, but we can control the rationalizations used in justifying the otherwise dishonest act. It is when we fail to do so, when we ultimately decide to lie to ourselves as well as others that we walk down the path of dishonesty and fraud.

4.6 CHAPTER HIGHLIGHTS

1. What is the first step in the decision making process?

The first step is to identify the facts of the given situation, realizing that we may not ever have all the facts, and the understanding of the facts we do have may be imperfect.

2. What is the second step in the decision making process?

The second step is to identify what the ethical problem may be.

3. What is the third step in the decision making process?

The third step is to identify all who may be affected by the issue and the decisions that we make.

4. What is the fourth step in the decision making process?

The fourth step is to consider possible options and alternatives.

5. What is the fifth step in the decision making process?

The fifth step is to actually make a decision.

6. After you have finished the fifth step in the decision making process, what if anything should you still do?

You should try to reexamine the decision made and learn from it.

7. What are the greatest motivators for dishonesty?

The greatest motivators for someone to act dishonestly are financial pressure and vices, specifically the perceived need for money.

8. What is one of the best ways to avoid rationalizing a situation?

One of the best ways to avoid rationalizing a situation is to call the action what it really is; i.e., it's not "payback", it's stealing.

PROBLEM FOR DISCUSSION

Megacorp has had a presence in Cityville for over fifty years. With over a thousand employees, it is by far the largest employer in the region. Over the last several years, the company has seen its profits begin to fall primarily due to competitive pressures. Specifically, its competitors have moved their plants overseas where labor costs are less than half of the labor costs of their previous U.S. operations. As such, the competitors have been able to price their product at a cost significantly lower than what Megacorp can charge. The general sense of the Board of Directors of Megacorp is that this is not a sustainable situation. One of the board members finally brings up the issue that no one really had wanted to talk about: is it time to close the operation in Cityville and move off shore so as to better compete in the market. Clearly the cost savings are there. If the move is made, over the next several years, profits of Megacorp are projected to increase dramatically. If the move is not made, Megacorp may still survive, but as a much smaller and dramatically less profitable company than it could otherwise be if the move is made. The board member proposing the move says that this isn't a tough choice. The numbers are there and the choice is obvious. You are a member of that board. Do you agree with the proposal? Is this really that simple of a choice? What is your decision making process?

CHAPTER FIVE

Corporate Social Responsibility

5.1 INTRODUCTION

Sooner or later, many of you will be working for a corporation. Some of you may be starting your own corporation someday. From the perspective of business ethics, no other business form has been more used, and, according to some, more abused, than the corporation. In this chapter we are going to look at what a corporation is, what its ethical role in society should be, and to whom do we look when there are ethical breaches committed by or in the name of a corporation.

5.2 WHAT IS A CORPORATION?

To understand the ethics of a corporation, it's important that we first understand what a corporation is. Barron's Dictionary of Finance and Investment Terms provides one of the better definitions of a corporation.

> Corporation: legal entity, chartered by a US, state or by the federal government, and separate and distinct from the persons who own it, giving rise to a jurist's remark that it has "neither a soul to damn nor a body to kick." Nonetheless, it is regarded by the courts as an artificial person; it may own property, incur debts, sue, or be sued.[1]

Let's take some of this definition apart, starting at its end. A corporation is an artificial person. It's not a real person. It's a creation of law. Although for many purposes we treat it as if it were a real person, (it can own property, enter contracts, etc.), it can't do what real people do. It can't vote. You do not go out to dinner with your corporation. You do not go on vacation with your corporation. In other words, it is a "person" only in so far as the law says it is a person, and only has such rights and powers as the law gives to it, nothing more, nothing less. Thus, Barron's is correct in saying that a corporation has no soul to damn nor body to kick. Only people have those attributes. By extension, not only does a corporation not have a soul nor a body, it also does not have a mind. So how does this soulless, bodiless, mindless entity do anything? Actually, it doesn't. Only people do something. People, its shareholders, generally own a corporation. They elect other people, a board of directors, to run the company. That board of directors may in turn hire other people, its officers and employees, to manage the day-to-day operations of the company. But regardless of titles, each step of the process involves people. One of the great lies told in business is that when an employee is terminated that it "was a corporate decision." There's no such thing. I guarantee you that there was some person with a name and a face who at some point in time drew a line through the terminated employee's name. So when we consider issues of corporate ethics and social responsibility, it is important to remember that each and every ethical challenge faced by a corporation is really being faced by people, its owners, its board of directors, its officers and mangers, and its employees.

5.3 WHAT IS THE ROLE OF A CORPORATION?

Now that we have an idea of what a corporation is, what is its purpose? There are two views that we will consider. The first is the so-called classical or economic view made famous by the late Nobel Prize winning economist Milton Friedman in his work, "Capitalism and Freedom." It is often simply called the shareholder view of corporations. The second view is far more expansive than the shareholder view. It is commonly referred to as the stakeholder view, emphasizing corporate social responsibility going far beyond the wants and needs of the company's shareholders. Let's begin with Friedman's shareholder view in his own words.

5.4 THE SHAREHOLDER VIEW OF CORPORATIONS

> The view has been gaining widespread acceptance that corporate officials...have a social responsibility that goes beyond serving the

---

1   Barron's Dictionary of Finance and Investment Terms, 4th ed, Downs and Goodman, NY, 1995

interests of their stockholders....This view shows a fundamental mis-
conception of the character and nature of a free economy. In such an
economy, *there is one and only one social responsibility of business-to use
its resources and engage in activities designed to increase its profits so long
as it stays within the rules of the game, which is to say, engages in open and
free competition, without deception or fraud*....(italics added)[2]

Friedman takes basically three concepts and weaves them together. First, ownership.
For Friedman, the shareholders are the owners of the enterprise. As such, any profits
made by the company rightfully belong to the people that own the company, the shareholders. And what of the board of directors and the management of the company? Here
is his second concept, agency. As you may remember, the shareholders elect the board
of directors, which in turn appoints the management. The Board is nothing more than
an agent for the shareholders, and management is nothing more than an agent of the
board. As any good agent should do, all of the agents' efforts should be expended in
serving the principal, which ultimately of course are the shareholders.

There is the classic example of charitable giving used to make the point. Is it appropriate for a member of the management of the company, on his or her own authority,
to make a charitable contribution of the company's funds? Friedman would argue that
it is not. Why? It is not that manager's money. That money belong to the owners, the
shareholders, and without their consent, the manager is violating his duty as an agent.
Put another way, feel free to give away as much of your own money as you want, but
don't go giving away mine.

Does this mean that in the pursuit of corporate profits, the company has no duty
to the other stakeholders that we talked about in the last chapter? Friedman would say
of course there are duties owed to these others, and we can easily identify those duties.
How? They're identified through the third concept woven into the process, contract.
The argument is pretty straightforward. Everything we do in business is a relationship
built on some form of mutual agreement, effectively a contract between the parties.
So what duties do we owe our employees? What does the contract say? For instance if
the company and the employee agree that the employee is to be paid twenty dollars
per hour for forty hours of work per week, that is the contract between the parties and
both sides have a duty to honor those terms, nothing more, nothing less. The same
contract analysis applies to all of the other stakeholders. Suppliers? Same idea. The
company will buy your supplies at an agreed upon price and you will provide the supplies when purchased. Is there any duty owed by either party after the purchase of the
supplies is made? No, the deal is complete. How about the local community? Nothing
changes. The company agrees to hire your citizens and pay your taxes and in return the
community will provide a place for the company to conduct its business.

For Friedman, the contract concept is at the heart of what he calls competitive capitalism or free enterprise. Two sides of a transaction enter into a deal voluntarily and
without coercion for their mutual benefit. Once an agreement is made, both parties
have a duty to honor it, again, nothing more, and nothing less.

2 Milton Friedman, Capitalism and Freedom, Chicago, University of Chicago Press, 1962 p. 133

But does this leave no place for ethics? Yes it does, in two places. First, in a most general sense, the ethics of value comes into place. What an individual may contract to buy or do is a reflection of their ethics. If for instance, in the exercise of your freedom, you contract to gamble away your money, this says as much about you and what you value as it does the activity. However, Friedman makes a more specific ethical comment. If we look at the quote from Friedman above, after he states the duty of a corporation is to make a profit he adds, *"so long as it stays within the rules of the game, which is to say, engages in open and free competition, without deception or fraud..."* By engaging in open and free competition, Friedman is talking about his concept of competitive capitalism stressing the concepts of voluntary agreement and mutual benefit. As to avoiding deception or fraud, Friedman seems to believe, reasonably, that most people know these things when they see them and no further explanation is necessary. (Friedman has been criticized on this last point as being overly simplistic as instances of business fraud and deception are not always so obvious. In fairness to Friedman, we should remember that he was writing a book on economics, not business ethics.)

So in somewhat of a nutshell form, this is the shareholder view of corporations. This view is certainly not shared by all. Over the last number of years, a second model of corporations has emerged. This is the stakeholder model emphasizing the concept of corporate social responsibility. Let's now take a look at this seemingly contradictory view.

5.5 THE STAKEHOLDER VIEW OF CORPORATIONS

As we said in Chapter Four, we are not islands. Our individual actions oftentimes affect a great deal more people than just ourselves. The same is true of a corporation. From a business perspective, every time a company does something, or decides not to do something, there is a perceived benefit to someone, and a cost to someone else. If we chose to hire Jones instead of Green, it is good for Jones and not so good for Green. If we build a plant in one city, that presumes we decided not to build it somewhere else. Going back to our end of chapter problem in Chapter Four, the issue of moving the business facility offshore, you hopefully remember all of the identified parties that are affected, some for the better and others for the worse. If we follow a strict interpretation of the shareholder view, the decision to do or not to do something is easy. Does the proposed action benefit the owners, the shareholders of the company, more than harm them? If yes, then the proposed action is justified regardless of how it may negatively affect anyone else. (Again, this presumes that we are staying within the rules of the game, which is to say, we are engaging in open and free competition, without deception or fraud.)

The stakeholder view soundly, and I might add, vehemently rejects this shareholder-centered view of corporations. The stakeholder view argues that the shareholder view is nothing more than an egoistic ethic, with a utilitarian structure only reined in by the law and the admonition of playing by the rules and not committing fraud or deception. It is a view of corporations that has lived well past its time and good riddance to it. The stakeholder view argues that because the actions of a corporation affect so many others, there is an ethical duty to take into account how a proposed action impacts all of those others, not just the shareholders. By way of review, remember who those "others" are: managers, employees, suppliers, customers, the local community, and yes, the shareholders. Note: The shareholders are considered just one of the many stakeholders in a corporation. They are the investors in the company without whom there would be no company and therefore are critical players in the corporation's success or failure. But isn't that true of the other stakeholders as well? A company is not going to do very well without its customers or suppliers. If there are not managers or employees to conduct the business, again, arguably that business is not long for survival. If the local community had not provided zoning, roads, utilities and the like, it's hard to see the operation being very successful. So if all of these stakeholders can legitimately claim a critical role in a company's success, what makes just one of those stakeholders, the shareholders so special? Under the stakeholder view, nothing. One of the better- known proponents of the stakeholder theory, Ed Freeman, put it as follows:

> The basic idea is that businesses and the executives who manage them, actually do and should create value for customers, suppliers, employees, communities, and financiers (or shareholders)...the primary responsibility of the executive is to create as much value for stakeholders as possible, and that no stakeholder interest is viable in isolation of the other stakeholders.[3]

For those of the stakeholder persuasion, it is not the role of management to do whatever it takes to increase profits for the shareholders, but rather to balance the interests of all stakeholders in the decision making process. Does this mean that managers must treat all stakeholders equally? Freeman says no.

> The stakeholder approach does not mean all stakeholders must be treated equally. Good managers must consider the concerns of all stakeholders, but then must prioritize those concerns based on the strategic purpose and values of the firm. One way to do this is examine the contributions, costs, and risks that a particular stakeholder group bears in relation to the strategic purpose of the firm.[4]

So what does this mean to all of you up and coming managers? If you subscribe to the stakeholder view, does this mean that you are forever condemned to a constant weighing and balancing and then prioritizing sometimes-competing stakeholder interests? Maybe. Isn't it a lot easier to simply ask does this proposal create shareholder value or not, regardless of how it affects anyone else? Probably. But is this how we want to do business? Is there a middle ground between the two views? Yes, or at least there should be.

---

3 "Managing for Stakeholders" by Edward Freeman in *Business Ethics: Decision Making for Personal Integrity and Social Justice,* by Laura Hartman and Joseph DesJardins, 2e, McGraw Hill, 2010
4 "Business Ethics A Managerial Approach", Wicks, Freeman, Werhane, Martin, Prentice Hall Person, NY 2010

5.6 THE REALITY VIEW

On its face it may look like the two views are more like opposing boxers where only one can leave the ring alive and there is no room for compromise. I would suggest that the two views are not as far apart as their proponents believe and suggest a third view to consider. This is what I call the "reality view" of a corporation. It primarily takes a longer-term look at a company and how its decisions may affect all of the stakeholders involved. It recognizes that in the short term, there will be winners and losers, but those winners and losers have to be evaluated in terms of determining first and foremost, the long term sustainability of the company. Consider the following. Presume that you are an adherent to the shareholder view, with shareholder profits being your ultimate driver. Question: How long do you think that the company is going to be profitable if your customers are unhappy? What if your suppliers decide not to deal with you anymore? How long will the business survive if you continue to lose employees because the company treats them so poorly? And for that matter, how long will a company survive if the shareholders are not making any money on their investment? Hopefully, you get the idea. This is the reality of business. If a company wants to prosper long term, it will out of necessity have to constantly take into consideration all of the other stakeholders involved in its ultimate success.

So what are you, as a manager to do? Under the reality view, first realize this simple truth: the goals of the shareholders are completely interwoven with the goals of the other stakeholders. But second, do not be naïve about the true role and position of the shareholders, the owners of the business. Are the shareholders really just one stakeholder among others? Is there really nothing special about the shareholders when compared to the other stakeholders? As a matter of fact and law, no, the shareholders are not just one stakeholder among others, and yes, they do occupy a special position in the stakeholder world. Although perhaps a bit egocentric, think of it this way. As an employee, or future employee, who has the power to hire, and I might add fire you? It is the shareholder group, the owners, (or their agents). By and large your immediate job and well-being depends on the good will of the owners of the company, and not necessarily any other stakeholder. Of course if you irritate the other stakeholders enough, they may influence the company's owners to take action against you, but again, that is up to the owners.

So as a future manager what should you do? I would suggest as follows. You will manage in such a way as to acknowledge the reality of the company's owners. They alone have the power to sign your paycheck or not and not the other stakeholders. However, with that being said, you will also manage in such a way as to keep the other stakeholders as happy as possible because you realize, once again, that the interests of the shareholders are interwoven with the interests of the stakeholders if the company looks to prosper long term. This is the reality view of corporations. If you remember this, you are well on your way to making good ethical and profitable decisions for your company. Does this mean that you will always be able to keep everyone happy? Not a chance. You will still have to weigh and balance competing interests in your decisions. But whether that process focuses on shareholder profits or stakeholder interests is, over the long term, not so relevant once we accept the reality of the fact that we are all in this together.

5.7 SOCIAL RESPONSIBILITY

Regardless of what view of corporations you decide to take, does a corporation have a social responsibility that goes beyond value creation to any of its immediate stakeholders? Yes, it does. This is no more apparent than in the case of environmental concerns. It would not be hard to think of a situation where the actions of the company result in significant value to all of its stakeholders, but at a social cost that very few of us would say is justified in paying. Say that the company wants to start a new manufacturing process that will greatly increase its production. Good for the shareholders in that they will make more money. The employees get more pay, the suppliers sell more supplies, more taxes are paid into the local community, and the managers all get raises. What's not to like? Well, part of the process redirects waste from the plant into the local river. Maybe not so much that in the short term anyone will really notice, but over the long term, it could be disastrous. What would you advise the company to do? Presuming that there is no ready solution at hand, the company very well may have to shelve their new process for now. Why? Because the corporation has a duty that goes beyond profits and goes to the well being of society both in the here and now and over time. From a pure shareholder view of corporations, this makes sense. If you want to sustain your company over the long term, the short-term profits that you think you are going to realize will in all likelihood vanish when it comes time to pay for the environmental disaster that you have created. From a stakeholder perspective this also makes sense. All of the benefits that you think you are going to get for everyone else will also not be sustainable over the long haul.

There is one other point to consider. Up to now, we have only discussed "primary stakeholders", those parties who are essential for the functioning of the corporation. Previously in Chapter Four we also mentioned secondary stakeholders. These would be anyone else that may claim to be affected by, or have an interest in the business, but without whom the business can by and large function without. Going back to our problem with the river waste, what of all of the people living along the river? Although they might not qualify as primary stakeholders, they certainly do have an interest in what the corporation is thinking about doing. This is what Milton Friedman called the "neighborhood effect", and no company can claim that they have no responsibility for how the company's actions affect these "neighbors".

Well, it could be argued, that if these people are harmed by the company's actions, they have the right to sue, to look to the law for a remedy. If the company is truly wrong then they will pay the legal cost, and that is true. But doesn't that ignore the moral issue? Remember when we talked about logical fallacies in Chapter Two? One of them was to confuse legality with morality. To argue that an action, such as polluting the river, is morally justified until a court tells you it is not sets the law up as the arbiter of ethics and morality. As we discussed, it is not. If you are still not sure what to do, go back to the decision making process that we talked about in our last chapter. Would you be comfortable with the decision to pour your waste into the river if you knew that this action would be widely reported in the press? Does your decision pass the "Mom test"? How does this decision make you feel? Does this decision pass the Golden Rule test? Does the decision pass the business vision test? Is this what you want your company to be known for? I would bet that almost all of you would conclude, based on these factors, dumping your plant's waste into the river is simply unacceptable, regardless of lost profits. And this example should tell us something else. Does a corporation have a social responsibility? You know, Mom knows, and society knows, it does.

5.8 RESPONSIBILITY FOR CORPORATE WRONGDOING

So whom do we hold responsible when something goes wrong? There are a couple of ways of looking at this. One approach is what we call the collectivist approach. It works like this. A corporation is first a collection of individuals. But it is more than that. It has certain attributes that individuals don't have. For example, a corporation can have perpetual existence. That is, people may come and go, but the corporate entity as established in law can go on forever. More so, a corporation has its own culture that is apart from the individuals that make it up. It is this corporate culture where things can go very wrong from an ethical perspective.

When we started this chapter we talked about how a corporation is an artificial person. It is not a real person. Yet, for anyone who has ever worked for a corporation of any size, you know that decisions made by managers often reflect more than just what that particular manager believes or wants to do. These decisions take place within a corporate culture and are a reflection of what some call its "corporate character." Consider the following quote:

> Although corporations always act through individual agents, and it is always an individual agent or group of agents who breaks the law, it is fair to say that corporations frequently *cause* (italics in original) the agents to violate the law. The behavior of individuals in corporations is not merely the product of individual choice; it is stimulated and shaped by goals, rules, policies, and procedures that are features of the corporation as an entity.[5]

It is these goals, rules, policies, and procedures, as well as the company's system of rewards and punishments that make up corporate character. Do you agree with this? Do you believe that it is possible for a corporation, due to its intangible corporate make up and character to be able to cause you to commit unethical acts? The other view says no. This is the individualist view of corporations.

This view goes back to the basic understanding that a corporation is an artificial person. It's not real. When someone knowingly commits an unethical act, there must be some intention to act unethically. Only real people, individuals, have to ability to

---

5 From Jennifer Moore, "Corporate Culpability Under the Federal Sentencing Guidelines," Arizona Law Review, 34, (1992) as printed in Ethical Theory and Business, Beauchamp and Bowie, 7th Ed, Prentice Hall, 2004 p100

intend anything. To claim that it was really the corporation's fault, it "made me do it" is nothing more than a rationalization, shifting agency, if you recall our list of rationalizations. In other words, you as an individual always have the ability, the choice, to say no. Without doubt the company can exercise a lot of influence, exert a lot of pressure, if you will, on what we decide to do, but ultimately the decision is ours. But let's be clear and honest about this. As our end of chapter case may show, that choice is oftentimes not an easy one to make and may come with a price if your decision goes against the culture of the company. But isn't this always true? The true test of character is choosing what is right, not what is easy.

5.9 CHAPTER HIGHLIGHTS

1. What is a corporation?

Corporation: legal entity, chartered by a US, state or by the federal government, and separate and distinct from the persons who own it, giving rise to a jurist's remark that it has "neither a soul to damn nor a body to kick." Nonetheless, it is regarded by the courts as an artificial person; it may own property, incur debts, sue, or be sued.

2. What are the two predominant views of the role of a corporation?

The first is the so-called classical or economic view made famous by the late Nobel Prize winning economist Milton Friedman in his work, "Capitalism and Freedom." It is often simply called the shareholder view of corporations. The second view is far more expansive than the shareholder view. It is commonly referred to as the stakeholder view, emphasizing corporate social responsibility going far beyond the wants and needs of the company's shareholders.

3. What is the role of a corporation under the shareholder view?

There is one and only one social responsibility of business: to use its resources and engage in activities designed to increase its profits so long as it stays within the rules of the game, which is to say, engages in open and free competition, without deception or fraud.

4. What is the role of a corporation under of the stakeholder view?

The primary responsibility of the corporation is to create as much value for stakeholders as possible, and that no stakeholder interest is viable in isolation of the other stakeholders, including shareholders.

5. What is an essential feature of the reality view of corporations?

Realize this simple truth: the goals of the shareholders are completely interwoven with the goals of the other stakeholders.

6. What do we mean by corporate social responsibility?

Regardless of what view of corporations you decide to take, a corporation has a social responsibility that goes beyond value creation to any of its immediate stakeholders.

7. What is the collectivist view of moral responsibility for wronging in a corporation?

The behavior of individuals in corporations is not merely the product of individual choice; it is stimulated and shaped by goals, rules, policies, and procedures that are features of the corporation as an entity, which can cause an employee to act unethically.

8. What is the individualist view of moral responsibility for wronging in a corporation?

This view goes back to the basic understanding that a corporation is an artificial person. To claim that it was really the corporation's fault, it "made me do it" is nothing more than a rationalization. You as an individual always have the ability, the choice, to say no.

PROBLEM FOR DISCUSSION

There was an accounting student who was just starting out on his first job after graduation. He was sent out as part of team to audit a company. He was given certain checklists to follow to ensure that all the correct audit procedures were followed. At the end of the day he went to his manager and told him that some of the procedures had not been done. The manager said not to worry about it and "sign off on them anyway." The student knew that this was not right. He also knew that if he refused, the manager would probably give him a poor review, which might cause him to lose his job. What should he do? His friends in the company told him that was the way the company operated, and he should just go along with it. It was, so to speak, the company's culture. Does he risk losing his job and say no? Or, is it really that he has no choice in the matter, and must go along with what he was told to do? What would be your decision?

CHAPTER SIX

Corporate Governance and Ethical Leadership

6.1 INTRODUCTION

Congratulations. You have now been made a director or an officer of Megacorp, Inc. You have now become the business leader that you always knew you would become. You are now part of the inner circle, part of corporate management, that is, corporate governance. So what have you gotten yourself into? From an ethical perspective, what obligations have you just undertaken? In this chapter we are going to discuss the three main and fairly general duties to which any officer and/or director of a corporation is subject. Additionally, we will identify additional duties that you also have, some of which are not only moral, but also legal. Let's start out discussing the general duties of officers and directors. In doing so, however, it is important to remember our discussion of corporations in our last chapter. Remember that a corporation is an artificial entity. It's a "let's pretend it's a person" sort of being. It only has such powers and rights as the law gives it. As such, when we discuss the first three duties of a corporation, it shouldn't come as a surprise that these duties, while most would certainly consider them to be moral duties, are also legal duties.

6.2 DUTY OF OBEDIENCE

Our first general duty is the duty of obedience. When we speak of the duty of obedience, we mean that you are not to act outside of the scope of the corporate purpose as it is defined in the company's Articles of Incorporation, or in violation of the laws of the state in which the company is incorporated. For instance, if the purpose of the corporation was defined in its Articles as being in the business of producing cream puffs, you cannot enter into a contract for the purchase of railroad cars. This would be unrelated and outside the scope of the purpose of the corporation. In technical legal terms, this is called an *ultra vires* act, that is, an act outside the power of the company.[1] Although this is rarely a legal issue today, there is an ethical issue to consider. That goes to the question of whether or not there is a duty of obedience to the fundamental mission statement of the company. A mission statement, or what some call a vision statement, is a statement about who you are, or more accurately, who or what the corporation is really all about. As an officer or director of the company, do you have a moral duty to be obedient to the principles that you have said define who and what you are? Most would say yes.

Consider the following examples of mission statements from various large U.S. corporations.

> **Becton, Dickinson and Company:** To help all people live healthy lives.
>
> **Bristol-Myers Squibb Company:** To discover, develop and deliver innovative medicines that help patients prevail over serious diseases.
>
> **Citigroup:** Our goal for Citigroup is to be the most respected global financial services company. Like any other public company, we're obligated to deliver profits and growth to our shareholders. Of equal importance is to deliver those profits and generate growth responsibly.
>
> **Dean Foods Corporation:** The Company's primary objective is to maximize long-term stockholder value, while adhering to the laws of the jurisdictions in which it operates and at all times observing the highest ethical standards.
>
> **HCA:** Above all else, we are committed to the care and improvement of human life. In recognition of this commitment, we strive to deliver high quality, cost effective healthcare in the communities we serve. In pursuit of our mission, we believe the following value statements are essential and timeless. We recognize and affirm the unique and intrinsic worth of each individual. We treat all those we serve with compassion and kindness. We act with absolute honesty, integrity and fairness in the way we conduct our business and the way we live our lives. We trust our colleagues as valuable members of our healthcare team and pledge to treat one another with loyalty, respect and dignity.

---

1 For the sake of accuracy, as a legal matter this issue rarely comes up today. Most modern companies state that the purpose of the corporation is "the transaction of any or all lawful businesses for which corporations may be incorporated" under the laws of the state in which they are incorporated. See Form BCA 2.10 Articles of Incorporation, Illinois Business Corporation act.

From this sampling of mission statements, we can see some common themes. Some speak of their mission in the broadest terms of helping people and society. Others speak of maximizing shareholder profits as its goal (Citigroup), but also doing so responsibly. Almost every mission statement that you will encounter acknowledges that even if the goal is profits, they take a second place to acting in an ethical and responsible manner. But isn't this just fluff? How do we know what acting in an ethical and responsible manner really means? One way to understand this is to go back to Chapter Four and review the section on "The Process" paying special attention to the nine factors listed in evaluating your options in the decision making process. Does this mean that our mission statement may go beyond any bare legal requirements? Yes, it may, but does that then mean that the mission statement can therefore be ignored, at least when it may be more convenient (read profitable) to do so? In other words, if the company is not legally required to respect the dignity of others, does that mean it doesn't have to if it doesn't want to for the sake of some other goal, such as increasing profits? Decide this for yourself. But if, as we said above, a mission statement is a statement about who and what you really and fundamentally are, following the mission statement may very well be a moral, if not a legal duty. Also remember the logical fallacy of confusing legality with morality. So unless you work for Murder, Inc., if you are facing a moral dilemma that seems to defy any quick solution, take a look at your mission statement. It may give you the guidance you need to make the best decision consistent with the values that you and your company say you aspire to.

6.3 DUTY OF LOYALTY

The duty of loyalty dictates that a director or corporate officer must act in good faith and must not allow his or her personal interests to prevail over the interests of the corporation.[2] Put another way, you have a duty to act first and foremost in the best interests of the corporation, and not what is first and foremost in your own personal self-interest. This is what's called subordination. You have a duty to subordinate your personal interests to the best interests of the company. This is not to say that many times what's in the best interests of the company is not also in your own best interest. Hopefully it usually will be, but not always. The most common ethical problem you will face here is the case of corporate bribery.

You are the purchasing manager of Megacorp. You have published an RFP (request for proposal) to take in bids to purchase a new piece of expensive equipment. The decision as to what bid to accept is ultimately yours. One of the companies that is bidding for the sale comes to you privately and lets you know that if you grant the bid to them, they will pay you a large sum of money to any bank account you designate. Also, known or unbeknownst to that company, you are experiencing severe personal financial difficulties, and you may lose your house and no longer be able to help your children with their college expenses. You have also noticed that over the past year your company's management has been ignoring you. You have received no pay raises in the last several years. So what do you do? On its face, this situation obviously violates your duty of loyalty to your company. So this case is an

---

2   Gearheart Industries v. Smith international, 741 F.2d 707, 719 (5th Cir 1984)

easy one, right? Remember the fraud triangle in Chapter Four? Here we have motivation, rationalization and opportunity. Will you be able to overcome these factors and abide by our duty of loyalty? Even if your need is great, you have a duty to subordinate your personal interests to the best interests of the company. And that's the hard part. It is not hard to turn down a bribe of money when you do not need the money. The challenge and the test of your integrity and loyalty come when you do need the money and are asked to put your interests ahead of the corporation.

6.4 DUTY OF CARE

The duty of care requires you to be diligent and prudent in managing the corporation's affairs. This does not mean that you can never make a mistake. In fact, under a principle of the law of corporations called the business judgment rule, you are not liable for losses incurred for decisions you make in good faith and in the exercise of reasonable care. What is reasonable care? That is the same level of care that any ordinary and reasonably prudent person in the same position would exercise. Remember that when you accept a job, any job, you have a duty to do that job as best you can, because that's more than likely what you told your employer that you would do. (Try getting through a job interview by saying that if the company hires you, you will perform to the least of your abilities and only do what is absolutely required of you to do. Good luck with that one.) Keeping your word is generally considered a moral duty, and as an officer and/or director of a company, exercising care in what you do is also a legal duty.

6.5 ETHICAL LEADERSHIP

We talked above about *what* to do in order to exercise good corporate governance. Now let's look at *how* you do this. Back in 1998, the Office of the Inspector General for the United States Department of Health and Human Services published seven guidelines for hospitals to follow to ensure that the hospitals were conducting themselves in both a legal and ethical manner. Specifically, the OIG said that one of the benefits to these guidelines was to "Concretely demonstrate to employees and the community at large the hospital's strong commitment to honest and responsible provider and corporate conduct."[3] As time went on, these seven guidelines have become the basic foundation for companies to follow in establishing themselves as minimally ethical companies and have come to be called by some, "The Seven Pillars of Compliance." Again, these are guidelines, and they are the minimum that we look for to see how a company is conducting itself. You will see that these are not totally soft guidelines, such as "do good and avoid evil." Instead, they are fairly practical, and that's why I said they really go to how you should be conducting your business. Now let's take a look at them. (Note: I have edited the OIG's document to show its applicability to all businesses, not just health care, and have tried to clean up the "government speak" in which the document was written.)

---

3 DEPARTMENT OF HEALTH AND HUMAN SERVICES, Office of Inspector General, Publication of the OIG Compliance Program Guidance for Hospitals Federal Register / Vol. 63, No. 35 / Monday, February 23, 1998 / Notices

6.6 THE SEVEN PRINCIPLES FOR CORPORATE CONDUCT

1. Written Policies and Procedures

Every company should require the development and distribution of written ethics policies that identify specific areas of ethical risk to the company. At a minimum, those policies should be provided to all individuals including the company's employees and independent contractors. In developing these policies the company should clearly address the basic *Standards of Conduct* that all employees, including management, are expected to follow. It's a good idea to involve high level company personnel in the development of these polices so that everyone down the chain of command knows that the policies are to be taken seriously.

Standards should state the organization's mission, goals, and ethical requirements of ethical compliance and give a clear statement of expectations for all employees, officers, managers, and, where appropriate, contractors and other agents. Standards should be distributed to, and made understandable to, all employees (e.g., translated into other languages and written at appropriate reading levels). Further, to assist in ensuring that employees continuously meet the expected high standards set forth in the code of conduct; any employee handbook describing or expanding upon these standards of conduct should be regularly updated as policies change over time.

At this point we should talk a bit about employee handbooks, as this can be a bit confusing. On one level, employee codes of conduct are considered different from the traditional employee handbook. The employee handbook might contain all of the practical and detailed policies governing your employment with the company. This might include dress codes, coming in late policies, vacation, disciplinary procedures, confidentiality agreements, statement of employee benefits, and the like. Some of these handbooks can be very extensive, or, if the company wants, not so much. A question that comes up regularly with employee handbooks is whether or not they are contracts between the company and the employee. The simple answer is it depends. Many, if not most such handbooks make it very clear in the handbook itself that the book is not to be considered a contract between the employee and the company. Thus, if the company violates a particular stated policy in the handbook to your detriment, can you hold the company liable for breach of contract? The answer is usually no, again, because the handbook has made it clear that it is not to be construed as a contract. However, if the company has not been clear on the nature of the handbook, it very well may be construed by a court as establishing a contractual relationship between you and your company and therefore could result in liability to the company for failure to follow the handbook provisions.

So does this mean that a company will have two different books—one book being its code of conduct the other being its employee handbook of company policy? Usually, not. The typical employee handbook usually incorporates the company's standards of ethical conduct into the handbook itself. So when you are hired by a company and provided with a copy of its handbook, be sure to read it. That can go a long way in keeping you out of trouble at your job and giving you some guidance as to what is expected of you.

2. The Designation of a Chief Compliance Officer and Other Appropriate Bodies, e.g., A Corporate Compliance Committee

This person or these persons have the responsibility of operating and monitoring the ethics compliance program, and they should report directly to the CEO and/or the company's Board of Directors. Over time this has resulted in most if not all publicly held corporations to create an ethics officer. Some of the duties of an ethics officer are as follows:

- Analyze the organization's industry environment and the legal requirements with which it must comply
- Assess existing policies and procedures that address these areas for possible incorporation into the ethics compliance program
- Work with appropriate company departments to develop standards of conduct and policies and procedures to promote compliance with the company's program
- Recommend and monitor the development of internal systems and controls to carry out the organization's standards, policies and procedures as part of its daily operations
- Determine the appropriate strategy/approach to promote compliance with the ethics program and detect any potential violations, such as through hotlines and other reporting mechanisms
- Develop a system to solicit, evaluate and respond to complaints and problems

Also note that the ethics officer reports either to the CEO of the company or directly to the Board of Directors. This assures that no one in the most senior management of the company is left out of the loop. Or, to put it in a perhaps slightly negative light, to prevent the directors or CEO of the company from later saying that they did not know about a particular ethical breach of conduct. In this light, any designated "ethics officer" should be of fairly high rank in the company. Designating the company mailroom clerk as ethics officer sends one message to the employees of the company. Designating a senior officer of the company as ethics officer sends quite another.

3. Conducting Effective Training and Education

The proper education and training of corporate officers, managers, and employees, and the continual retraining of current personnel at all levels, are significant elements of an effective ethics compliance program. As part of their compliance programs, companies should require personnel to attend specific training on a periodic basis, including appropriate training in corporate and legal policies and training in corporate ethics.

The organization must take steps to communicate effectively its standards and procedures to all affected employees, such as by requiring participation in training programs and distributing publications that explain in a practical manner specific ethical requirements. Managers of specific departments or groups can assist in identifying areas that require training and in carrying out such training. Training instructors may come from outside or inside the organization. New employees should be targeted for training early in their employment. The ethics officer should document any formal training undertaken by the company as part of the compliance program.

The company can use a variety of teaching methods. Note that in companies where there is a great deal of cultural diversity, especially in terms of language, the company should provide language specific training for those employees who may not be fluent in English so that all employees are knowledgeable of the institution's standards of conduct and procedures for alerting senior management to problems and concerns.

It is recommended that attendance and participation in training programs be made a condition of continued employment. If an employee does not comply with the company's training requirements that should result in disciplinary action, including possible termination, when such non-compliance is serious. Following the provisions of the ethics compliance program, such as training requirements, should be a factor in the annual evaluation of each employee.

4. Developing Effective Lines of Communication

Access to the Ethics Officer: An open line of communication between the ethics officer and company personnel is equally important to the successful implementation of an ethics program and the reduction of any potential for unethical conduct. Written confidentiality and non-retaliation policies should be developed and distributed to all employees to encourage communication and the reporting of incidents of ethical violations. The ethics officer should also develop several independent reporting paths for an employee to report unethical conduct so that supervisors or other personnel cannot divert such reports. For example, if it is the policy of your company to report unethical conduct to your immediate supervisor, what do you do if it is your immediate supervisor who in fact is committing the unethical act? A good plan will provide a way around this.

The company should set up a procedure so that personnel may seek clarification from the ethics officer if there is any confusion or question with regard to company policy or procedure. The ethics officer may want to ask for employee input in developing these communications and reporting systems.

Hotlines and Other Forms of Communication: The use of hotlines (including anonymous hotlines), e-mails, written memoranda, newsletters, and other forms of communication can be used to maintain open lines of communication. If the company establishes a hotline, the telephone number should be made readily available to all employees and independent contractors, possibly by conspicuously posting it on the telephones in common work areas. Employees should be permitted to report matters on an anonymous basis. Matters reported through the hotline or other communication sources that suggest substantial violations of ethics policies, regulations or law should be documented and investigated promptly to determine their veracity. A log should be maintained by the ethics officer that records such calls, including the nature of any investigation and its results. Such information should be included in reports to the Board of Directors and/or the CEO. Further, while the company should always strive to maintain the confidentiality of an employee's identity, it should also explicitly communicate that there may be a point where the individual's identity may become known or may have to be revealed in certain instances, especially if outside parties such as law enforcement become involved. Does this mean that you cannot always guarantee complete anonymity to an employee who lodges a complaint? Yes, it does. In extreme cases you cannot make that guarantee.

Sooner or later you are going to deal with this problem. You are going to be in a situation where you see a co-worker engaging in clearly unethical if not outright illegal activities. As a practical matter it can be a very hard thing to "blow the whistle", to turn the individual in to the company. But look at it this way. Dishonesty or unethical acts committed by one person reflects ultimately on all the persons that make up the company including you. What does it say about your own moral makeup that if you see clear wrongdoing you simple turn away and ignore it? The old adage is still true: the only thing necessary for the triumph of evil is that good men (and women) do nothing. Sooner or later the chances of the co-worker getting caught are very high. When it comes out that you knew about it long ago and said or did nothing about it, your career with that company may come to a rapid end, as well it should.

5. Enforcing Standards Through Well-Publicized Disciplinary Guidelines

Discipline Policy and Action: An effective ethics program should include guidance regarding disciplinary action for corporate officers, managers, and employees who have failed to comply with the company's standards of conduct, policies and procedures, or those who have otherwise engaged in wrongdoing, which has the potential to harm the company's status as a reliable, honest and trustworthy company.

The company should include a written policy statement setting forth the degrees of disciplinary actions that may be imposed upon corporate officers, managers, and employees for failing to comply with the company's standards and policies. Intentional or reckless noncompliance should subject transgressors to significant sanctions. Such sanctions could range from oral warnings to suspension or termination as appropriate. The written standards of conduct should explain the procedures for handling disciplinary problems and those who will be responsible for taking appropriate action. Department managers can handle some disciplinary actions, while others may have to be resolved by senior personnel. Disciplinary action may be appropriate where a responsible employee's failure to detect a violation is attributable to his or her negligence or reckless conduct. The company should tell personnel that disciplinary action will be taken on a fair and equitable basis. Managers and supervisors should be made aware that they have a responsibility to discipline employees in an appropriate and consistent manner.

It is important to publish the range of disciplinary standards for improper conduct and to educate officers and other employees regarding these standards. The consequences of noncompliance should be consistently applied and enforced, in order for the disciplinary policy to have the required deterrent effect. All levels of employees should be subject to the same disciplinary action for the commission of similar offenses. The commitment to ethical behavior applies to all personnel levels within the organization.

6. Auditing and Monitoring

An ongoing evaluation process is critical to a successful ethics program. This should include regular reporting to the Board of Directors and/or the CEO. An effective program should also incorporate periodic (at least annual) reviews of whether the program's compliance elements have been satisfied, e.g., whether there has been appropriate dissemination of the program's standards, training, ongoing educational programs and disciplinary actions, among others. This process will verify actual conformance by all departments with the ethics program. As part of the review process, the ethics officer should consider techniques such as interviews with personnel involved in management and operations and/or questionnaires developed to solicit impressions of a broad cross-section of the company's employees and staff. After any such review, the findings should be presented to the Board of Directors and/or the CEO on a regular basis.

7. Responding to Detected Offenses and Developing Corrective Action Initiatives

Violations and Investigations: Violations of a company's ethics program and other types of misconduct threaten a company's status as a reliable, honest and trustworthy organization. Detected but uncorrected misconduct can seriously endanger the mission, reputation, and even the legal status of the company. Consequently, upon reports or reasonable indications of suspected wrongdoing, it is important that the ethics officer or other management officials initiate prompt steps to investigate the conduct in question to determine whether a material violation of applicable law or the requirements of the ethics compliance program has occurred, and if so, take steps to correct the problem.

These are the so-called Seven Pillars. Should each of these be applied in every company? Obviously that is going to depend on the size and nature of the company. A small company may not have a dedicated ethics officer. However, that does not mean that there should not be someone of authority that can fulfill that role along with his or her other duties. As a practical matter, even in a smaller company, if you were the CEO, would you really not want to know if an employee of yours was committing fraud, employee theft, misrepresenting your product to customers or engaging in other unethical actions? (Hint: if you answered no, you would rather not know, things will get a lot easier for you. Your company, however small, won't be around very long so you will not have to worry about it.)

Finally, there is one last reason to take these seven principles seriously. They may keep you out of jail. The Federal Sentencing Guidelines say that any person or organization is liable to sentencing including prison, fines, and to periods of probation for federal offenses connected with antitrust, securities, bribery, fraud, money laundering, criminal business activities, extortion and embezzlement, conspiracy, and other wrongful acts. If you find yourself caught up in this situation and are convicted of an offense, The Federal Sentencing Guidelines give a wide range of possible penalties to which you can be subject. And it may not help you to say that, well, the corporation committed the offense, you were just an employee/agent of the company. The Guidelines say not only can the court fine the corporation millions of dollars, but you, as its agent could be sentenced to up to three years in federal prison and also be liable for millions of dollars in fines. One way to mitigate your sentencing, or that of the company, is to have an "effective compliance program" as outlined above. Here's the rule. In order to reduce penalties under the Federal Sentencing Guidelines:

> an organization shall-
>
> (1) exercise due diligence to prevent and detect criminal conduct; and
> (2) otherwise promote an organizational culture that encourages ethical conduct and a commitment to compliance with the law.
>
> Such compliance and ethics program shall be reasonably designed, implemented, and enforced so that the program is generally effective in preventing and detecting criminal conduct. The failure to prevent or detect the instant offense does not necessarily mean that the program is not generally effective in preventing and detecting criminal conduct.[4]

What does that compliance and ethics program look like? The "Seven Pillars" we talked about above with perhaps one modification. The Sentencing Guidelines lump together communication and education and add "The organization shall use reasonable efforts not to include within the substantial authority personnel of the organization any individual whom the organization knew, or should have known through the exercise of due diligence, has engaged in illegal activities or other conduct inconsistent with an effective compliance and ethics program."[5] In other words, the company should not hire the fox to watch the chickens. You have to exercise due diligence, that is, be very careful, when delegating authority to anyone who may have questionable ethical standards or be of doubtful ethical character. So apart from just being good business practice, following these principles may go a long way in helping you avoid sharing a jail cell with a guy named Spike.

6.7 CHAPTER HIGHLIGHTS

1. What do we mean by the "duty of obedience?"

When we speak of the duty of obedience, we mean that you are not to act outside of the scope of the corporate purpose as is defined in the company's Articles of Incorporation, or in violation of the laws of the state in which the company is incorporated.

2. Do you have a duty of obedience to a company's mission statement?

If a mission statement is a statement about who and what you really and fundamentally are, following the mission statement may very well be a moral, if not a legal duty.

3. What is the duty of loyalty?

The duty of loyalty dictates that a director must act in good faith and must not allow his or her personal interests to prevail over the interests of the corporation.

---

4   Federal Sentencing Guidelines, Chapter Eight, Section 8B2.1
5   IBID

4. What is the duty of care?

The duty of care requires you to be diligent and prudent in managing the corporation's affairs.

5. What are the Seven Pillars of Corporate Compliance?

1. Have written policies and procedures.
2. Designate a chief compliance officer or ethics officer or other appropriate body.
3. Conduct effective ethics training and education.
4. Develop effective lines of communication.
5. Enforce Standards Through Well-Publicized Disciplinary Guidelines.
6. Audit and monitor the activities, progress and success of the ethics program.
7. Respond to detected offenses and develop corrective action initiatives.

6. Can I as an employee of a company that is convicted of wrongdoing under the Federal Sentencing Guidelines be personally subject to fines or prison?

Yes. You are considered an agent of the employer and you individually can have personal liability under the Guidelines, which includes fines and imprisonment.

7. Is there any way to lessen a sentence under the Federal Sentencing Guidelines?

Yes. A company having an effective compliance program, such as the Seven Pillars, may mitigate its sentence under the law. This is true even if the program failed to detect the wrongful act in question.

PROBLEM FOR DISCUSSION

Green Corporation has had its eye on Black Corporation for some time with thoughts of acquiring Black. Seeing that the price of Black's stock was down to $37 a share, the CEO of Green, Mr. Jones, approached the CEO of Black, Mr. Smith, over dinner and said that Green would acquire Black for $55 per share, an obvious high premium over the current stock price. Smith immediately told Jones that Smith thought the offer was more than fair, and that he would recommend that his Board of Directors accept the offer and recommend that its shareholders do the same. Smith, without doing any detailed research into the actual valuation of his company, or asking Jones what Jones based the $55 offer price on, did as he promised. After some discussion with his Board, the Board in fact did approve the sale. Some of the shareholders of Black Corporation were upset over the deal, and claimed that the price of $55 was only about 60 percent of what the company was really worth. In defense of his and the Board's action, Smith invoked the business judgment rule and said that even if the company was worth a lot more than $55, neither he nor the Board had any liability for their actions. Do you agree?

CHAPTER SEVEN

Moral Rights in the Workplace

7.1 INTRODUCTION

Webster defines "work" as: "the labor, task, or duty that is one's accustomed means of livelihood." Except for those of us have been born rich, just about everyone else has to work in order to make a living. As a general proposition, people are going to fall into one of two categories. They are either going to be employers, or they are going to be employees. In this chapter we are concerned with what happens to most of us, that is, being an employee.

For those of you that have some experience in this position, it comes as no surprise that the day you started your first job was the day that you lost a lot of your ability to control your own life. Now you have a boss. There is now someone who is going to tell you what to do, how to do it and when it has to be done. He or she may or may not care to hear your problems or why you were late to work or why you were not able to get some assignment done the way he wanted it and when he wanted it. For most employees you are what is called an "employee at will." More on this shortly, but simply put, if the boss isn't happy with you, you're fired. But is it really that sadly simple? Is your life solely up to the whims of the boss? Fortunately the answer is no, at least to some extent. This chapter is going to look at some of the rights that you as an employee may or may not have when you enter the workforce. These rights are going to come from two sources; legal rights and protections as granted under law, and ethical rights and duties that any company claiming an ethical basis should follow. As we go over this material, keep in mind the larger picture. That is, don't just look at this from the perspective of what your boss or supervisor can and cannot do to you. Remember that as time goes on, you very well may be the boss of someone else, and you want to know what you as a future supervisor can and cannot do to your employees.

7.2 RIGHT TO WORK

Any discussion of rights in the workplace starts with a fundamental question: do you have a right to a job or employment in the first place? To answer this question we first have to separate out a few concepts to really understand what is happening here. First, don't confuse the concept of "right to work" as an ethical concept and right to work as a legal concept. Let's begin with the ethical concept of right to work.

Do you have a right to work? The United Nations Universal Declaration of Human Rights states:

> **Article 23.**
> (1) Everyone has the right to work, to free choice of employment, to just and favorable conditions of work and to protection against unemployment.

So there you have it. The United Nations clearly says that yes, you do have a right to work. Subject closed? Maybe not so fast.

Whenever anyone claims a right or some body recognizes something as a right, this creates a corresponding duty on someone else. For example, if we say that children have a right to an elementary education that creates a positive duty on someone, in this case society, to provide that education. Or in the negative sense, if we say that you have a right to free speech that creates a negative duty on someone else not to interfere with that right. So following out the logic, if we say that you have a right to work that implies that someone or something has a duty to provide you with that work. Who might that someone or something be? There are only a few possibilities.

First, there is private business. Does it make sense to say that a private company must offer work to anyone who asks for it? Obviously not. Not only does this ignore the problem of job qualifications, but the basic reality that if a company only needs one hundred employees at its facility, requiring it to hire more than that would not only be inefficient, but could sooner or later put the company out of business. More so, requiring a company to hire somebody, anybody, arguably infringes on a company's property rights. This is especially true under the shareholder model. You are the owner of the company. As such, at least to some extent, you have the right to do what you want with your company, including the right to decide who will and will not work for you. I do want to add, however, that this right is not unrestricted, both from an ethical and legal point of view. Respect for human dignity requires that you do not discriminate in your hiring decisions. (Additionally, as we will see in Chapter Eight, the law also prevents discrimination in hiring based on various criteria.) If the company is in the market to hire someone, all applicants must be given an equal opportunity to fill that job opening. However, providing equal employment opportunity to qualified applicants is a far different matter than requiring a company to hire someone simply because that person wants a job. This would be unworkable. So no, the private sector is not a place to go for guaranteed employment.

Second, there is the public sector, or if you will, the government. If the private sector cannot be required to provide employment to everyone who seeks a job, should, or can, that duty be assumed by the government? To some degree, the problems with looking to the public sector to accomplish full employment are the same as looking to the private sector to do so. We can assume that government jobs also require certain qualifications. For instance, if the government needs employees for governmental accounting, presumably anyone the government hires would have some training or qualification in accounting. Likewise, from an efficiency perspective, if a particular government agency needs one thousand employees to do its job, does it make sense for that agency to be required to hire any more than that number? However, there are clear differences between the public and the private sector. First, the missions are different. In the broadest sense, the mission of a private sector company is to make a profit. The mission of government is to provide services for its citizens, without being hindered (at least to a large extent) by quarterly profit and loss statements. Raising prices to customers may not always be a viable alternative for a company needing to increase its revenue in a competitive environment. Government on the other hand has the power of taxation as well as certain other abilities that it can use to raise as much money as it needs to fund its operations. (The Federal government, for example, owns its own mint. It can print the money if it has to.) More so, the government has the ability to create jobs if necessary to directly deal with the problem of chronic unemployment.[1] But is that a good solution? As the government has no need to worry about profits and return to shareholders, it can provide services far more cheaply than the private sector. So what's wrong with that? Simply put, no private sector company could compete with the government. As a result, private businesses would quickly fail, and its now unemployed workers would themselves become government workers, and the private enterprise system would be in significant jeopardy. So it does not appear that the government can take on this role any better than the private sector can do so.

So what do we do? Virtually every basic requirement of life, food, clothing, shelter, all comes with a price. They are not free. To avail oneself of even these most basic necessities means that you need a job to earn the money necessary to pay for these things. In order to argue there is no right to a job may be saying that you have no right to the basic necessities of life. And if that is true, are we not saying that you therefore have no right to life itself? Here is where we are with this today. As a matter of policy, and perhaps reality, it is clear that an individual does not have a specific right to employment. At best, one has the right to equal opportunity of being employed, but again, no guaranteed right to an actual job. The current policy of the U.S. is to provide for safety nets for the unemployed and others who are distressed. This takes the form

---

1 The best example of this was the creation of the Civilian Conservation Corp which operated between 1933 and 1942. During its existence, it provided up to 2.5 million jobs to unemployed depression era citizens.

of unemployment compensation, certain welfare programs and the like. Is this the good solution? Few would argue that it is, but lacking other avenues of employment opportunity for many, that is the best that we can come up with for now.

For the sake of completeness and clarity, I want to briefly mention what "right to work" means in a legal context. If you are in a so-called right to work state, you cannot be forced to join or stay in a union that may exist in your place of employment. That also means that you cannot be forced to pay union dues if you opt out of the union, nor can your employer or the union pressure or otherwise coerce you into joining the union. Specific rules in right to work states vary according to the state in which you reside, and overall by my last count twenty-three of the states are currently right to work jurisdictions. Whether right to work laws are ethically valid is a topic of high debate. One the one hand, proponents of right to work laws argue that a person's freedom of association, that is, your right to join or not join, be affiliated or not affiliated with any group, organization, or other individual for that matter, is a fundamental right of the individual. More so, requiring employees to be in a union and pay union dues may be forcing them to support political or even moral positions that they do not personally endorse. This is typically seen in cases where national unions contribute large sums of money to a particular political party or candidate that the individual union member may not support. There are also economic arguments made in favor of right to work laws as being a benefit to business and overall employment. Although I will not be addressing those economic arguments here, be assured that they are hotly disputed by those who are opposed to right to work laws.

On the other hand, opponents of right to work laws argue that it is almost undisputed that wages and benefits for unionized workers are higher and better than those of non-union companies. Thus, if you work for a unionized company, the union negotiates pay and benefit packages for all of the workers of the company, those in the union and those who chose not to join the union. This results in what is called the free-rider problem. The short explanation to this is that it is unfair for someone to take the benefit of others' work without paying for it. In the collective bargaining context, the workers who decide not to be in the union, and not pay union dues, nevertheless get the benefits of being in the union as whatever contract is ultimately negotiated between the union and the company benefits the non-union workers just as if they were part of the union. And the advantages go beyond wages and benefits. They also may include job health and safety rules and other non-economic benefits. Further, there is the practical argument given. Collective bargaining is far more effective in assuring or gaining job benefits than would the actions of individual employees trying to negotiate their separate agreements with the company. I do not propose to settle this debate here. However, as business students you should think about this issue and ask yourselves if even from a utilitarian perspective, right to work laws make sense.

7.3 EMPLOYMENT AT WILL

The doctrine of employment at will states that if there is no employment contract or law to the contrary, employers have the right to hire, promote, demote or fire any employee at any time, for any reason, including no reason. And this is a two way street. An employee can quit whenever he or she wants for any reason, including no reason. This is not as straightforward as it seems. For example, according to data from the National Conference of State Legislatures, as of 2008, only three states are pure employment at will states: Florida, Georgia and Rhode Island. All other states have some types of exceptions to the general doctrine. For example, if an employee is fired solely based on race that would be a violation of either the law of a given state or the public policy of that state, not to mention federal law. However, for our purposes here, let's look at the general doctrine and talk about if it makes ethical sense.

Why does this doctrine exist at all? On its face it seems that an employee should have some recourse before he or she is fired, especially if that firing is what we call "without cause", meaning I am firing you simply because I can. Patricia Werhane and Tara Radin have spent some time looking at this issue, and here are some of the arguments in favor of this doctrine and some of the counter arguments to those.[2]

First, there is the property right argument. The owner of the business is just that, the owner. It's my business, my property if you will, and I have a right to do with it as I so choose. If I want to sell it I can. If I want to close it down I can. And if I want to throw out an asset that I do not want any more, like you for instance, I can do that too. Don't like it? Start your own business or go work somewhere else.

Seems a bit harsh, but this is the property right argument. Is this an ethical position? Many, including myself, would argue that it is not. Remember Kant back in Chapter Three? He said that we may never treat other people as merely some means to fulfill our own personal (or business) ends. Rather, other people must be treated as being ends in themselves. In the context of the property right argument for employment at will it comes down to this: people, employees, are simply not property that you can dispose of simply because you can. They are ends in themselves and worthy of respect for their own human dignity.

Second, there is the freedom of contract argument. Both the employer and the employee have a right to negotiate any deal that they want. If you don't like an employment at will situation, part of the bargaining process between you and the employer might include a provision or agreement that exempts you from this situation. More so, as a matter of contract, if you are in an employment at will situation, you know that, and no one made you take the job. So you have nothing to complain about.

On its face, this seems to be a pretty fair argument and in an ideal world of employment, we might go along with this. The problem is that we seldom find ourselves in an ideal employment world. How many employees are really in a position where they can actually negotiate their employment situation? Negotiation implies that both sides have some leverage over the other. I have something that I really want to sell, and you have something that you really want to buy. In this case, we can negotiate as both parties to the deal have something the other party really wants. Is this how it works for most employees? Probably not. The hard reality of most employment situations is that it is a pretty one sided deal, and that's on the side of the employer. The employee usually simply does not have sufficient leverage, if any leverage at all, to negotiate a deal with the employer. Unless the employee has a specialized skill really needed by the

---

2 Werhane, Patricia, and Tara Radin, 32004, "Employment and Employee Rights", Malden, MA, Blackwell

employer, or we are in an era of very low unemployment, the employee is generally in a take it or leave it situation. In other words, when it comes to freedom of contract, how much freedom does the employee actually have to negotiate anything beyond what the employer is offering? If the answer to that question is little to none, then this freedom of contract argument fails.

A third argument is one based on practicality. It goes something like this. If an employer was required to show cause, that is, give a reason when it wants to terminate an employee that the employer felt was not performing, that would result in a lengthy and time consuming process that is both costly and inefficient. (We will talk more about "process" in a few moments.) Is this a valid argument? On its face, yes. We have all heard the stories of certain public sector employees who have extensive so called due process rights that have to be followed in order for them to be terminated. In some cases, the process could literally take years and cost massive amounts of money.[3] Is this the sort of thing that we want to saddle businesses with? Many would argue no.

But let's look closer at this problem. Once again we have to remember that employees are people and as such have a human dignity that ought to be respected by others. Part of those "others" is the employer. Further, recalling our discussion of Emmanuel Kant, people are not to be used simply as a means to your own end. Rather, we have to remember that they are ends in themselves. Thus, when any employer decides to act in such a way as to significantly and negatively impact the lives of his employees, he has an ethical duty to ensure that the action being contemplated meets the basic requirements of justice. That is, that the action reflects the humanity of the person or persons being affected. Does that come with a cost to the employer? Yes, it does. However, this should simply be viewed as a cost of doing business similar to the costs incurred by the business in hiring the employee to begin with.

At this point hopefully most of us would probably agree that an employee should not be terminated for no reason whatsoever, except for the fact that the employer may have the legal right to do so. So what does this mean as a practical matter in a company? It means that employees should have some rights to what we call "due process."

The concept is well rooted in the United States Constitution, which says that no one is to be deprived of life, liberty or property without "due process of law." Of course this Constitutional protection does not apply to non-government activities, but the principle is the same. If you have a job, the argument goes that you should not be deprived of that job, similar to a property right, without some due process. This is not as complicated as it sounds. There are two aspects to due process. The first is procedural due process. What this requires is that there is some reasonable mechanism in place that an aggrieved party can look to in order to find some redress for his or her complaint. For example, let's say that your superior does not like the color of the tie that you wore to work today. In a pure employment at work situation, the supervisor arguably could terminate your

---

3 New York Post, January 29, 2012, "Disgraced teacher is worth $10M, makes $100,000 a year, does nothing, & refuses to leave." Story in part states: "Deemed a danger to kids, the typing teacher …hasn't been allowed in a classroom for more than a decade, but still collects $100,049 a year in city salary — plus health benefits, a growing pension nest egg, vacation and sick pay. Mayor Bloomberg and Gov. Cuomo can call for better teacher evaluations until they're blue-faced, but Rosenfeld (the teacher) and six peers with similar gigs costing about $650,000 a year in total salaries are untouchable. Under a system shackled by protections for tenured teachers, they can't be fired, the DOE says." By SUSAN EDELMAN

employment. If you have some procedural due process rights that means that there is some mechanism that you can use to appeal what is clearly an arbitrary and unjust decision. What that mechanism may be will vary wildly from company to company. It may be something as simple as being able to go in and talk to a more senior person in the company, to a more elaborate formal hearing situation as established by the company. Regardless, some mechanism should exist.

The second aspect of due process is what we call substantive due process. In its broadest sense substantive due process means that after availing yourself of the procedural processes that are (hopefully) in place, you are entitled to some rational explanation and result. Now some would argue that whether a result is "rational" more often than not seems to depend upon which side of the decision you come down on. If the decision of the process is that the employee was wrongfully terminated, the employee will probably conclude that in fact this was a truly rational decision. Of course if the decision goes the other way, the employee might conclude that the decision was something less than rational. Is it really that cynical of a result? Maybe not. I would suggest this. When considering the substance of a decision, look to see if it is principle based. By that I mean, does it appear that concepts of fundamental fairness and equality of treatment have been applied? Does the punishment of termination fit the offense? Has the employee been given a real opportunity to present his side of the story? Bearing in mind that neither process, procedural or substantive, is ever going to be perfect and please everyone involved, at least if you test the decision by these basic principles, you should feel reasonably confident that your decision is indeed rational.

7.4 CONTRACT RIGHTS

The above discussion on employment at will and due process concerned itself primarily with issues involving your moral rights as an employee. We should also spend a few moments talking about what contract rights you may have as an employee, if any. I say "if any" because this discussion presupposes that you have a contract with your employer to begin with. Most employees do not. However, if you are offered a contract of employment, there are a few things that you should be aware of.

Almost by definition a contract between you and your employer is a negotiation. The employer wants you, or at least your skill set, and you want to provide the same to the employer. When you sit down across the table with your prospective employer, remember that everything is up for discussion. That includes salary, vacation, fringe benefits and just about anything else you or the employer wants to put into the agreement. As this is not a book on Business Law, I will leave the particulars of how contracts work to either your Business Law class or your lawyer. That being said, there are a couple of issues that you do want to be particularly aware of, especially as they touch upon some ethical considerations. They are covenants not to compete and confidentiality agreements.

A covenant not to compete is usually part of an employment contract where the employee agrees that he or she will not work for any competitor of the current (or prospective) employer for specified periods. For a long time it was argued that these types of agreements should not be legally enforceable in that they restrain an employee's ability to make a living if the employee leaves the current position for any reason, including being fired. As you remember from our discussion above as to whether a person has a basic right to work at all, (the answer in the United States is no), these agreements have generally been enforced by the courts. However, there are some qualifications. First you, the employee, must receive some consideration, something of value, from the employer in return for agreeing to enter into the covenant not to compete. This requirement is usually met with the offer of the job itself. Second, the terms of the covenant must pass the reasonability test. That means that they must be reasonable in three areas: time, territory and legitimate business interest. If, for instance, the covenant said that you could not work for any competitor of the employer for a period of twenty years anywhere within the United States, most courts would find that unreasonable both in terms of the time of the covenant as well as the geographic area covered. This of course depends on what your position in the company was, but by and large, except for the unusual cases, the time and territory of these agreements should be relatively short and limited. Thus, you lose your job as a marketing executive for your company. If your covenant said you could not work for any other firm in the same industry for one year and within the City of Chicago, this would probably be upheld. The covenant must also protect a legitimate business interest of the employer. If you were that marketing exec for a company, that company probably has a legitimate business interest in you not jumping ship to work for a competitor due to your experience and expertise. However, if your job was pumping gas at a service station, even though the covenant might be reasonable in terms of time and territory, it is hard to imagine any legitimate business interest of the employer needing to be protected.[4] However, like any other contract term, if you see this, it is also subject to negotiation.

Oftentimes coupled right along with the covenant not to compete is a confidentiality agreement, or what some call a non-disclosure agreement. Originally based on the concept of an employee's duty of loyalty (see Chapter Six), today these agreements are usually a separate and written agreement between the employer and the employee. In its simplest form, the employee agrees not to disclose to anyone, either during his employment or for a period thereafter, any confidential or proprietary information of the current employer. This information usually includes client lists, financial information, trade secrets, business plans, and confidential production techniques and just about anything else that an employer may list. Both a legal and ethical problem occurs when a competitor of your employer wants to hire you away from your current job (presuming no covenant not to compete problems) precisely because you have this sort of knowledge. Do you take the job, with its large pay increase, and tell you new employer all of your now former employer's secrets? From the ethical perspective, the answer must be no. You gave your word not to disclose this information and keeping your word is generally considered a moral obligation. Not convinced? All right, from a legal perspective you have violated your confidentiality agreement and that comes with negative legal (read money or worse) consequences. So be it a covenant not to compete or

---

4 For the sake of completeness, know that the law covering the enforceability of covenants not to compete varies from state to state. If you are not sure whether the covenant being offered to you is reasonable and enforceable in your state, check with a lawyer.

a confidentiality agreement, know what you are agreeing to at the time and recognize that both have ethical and legal consequences.

7.5 HEALTH AND SAFETY

Do you as an employee have a right to work in a safe and healthy workplace environment? On its face this looks like a no-brainer. Of course, you do. Who would argue with that? However, upon closer examination, we may find that this is not so easy of a question. Let's first take a look at the real issue: that is, what is meant by a safe environment?

From the outset, let's come to the understanding that there is no such thing as a completely safe work environment. Some might argue that there is no such thing as a completely safe anything. (People have been known to fall out of their own beds.) So to say that any employee has a right to a completely safe work environment is an impossible goal to achieve. Of course this does not mean that we simply throw up our hands and say "good luck" to our employees. Instead, we have to decide what risks are acceptable and what risks are not. I would suggest a twofold analysis of risk, and this can be applied to any activity in which we engage. First, what is the probability of being harmed? And we can look at harm in as broad a context as we like. Harm can by physical, economic, psychological and/or a combination of all three. For example, we all know that there is some risk to travelling in a car. If you are driving on an open road with little traffic on a clear day, you might conclude, if you thought about it at all, that you have less than a one percent chance of getting into a harmful accident. On the other hand the likelihood of getting into an accident may go up dramatically if you find yourself driving in a terrible snowstorm, at midnight, surrounded by other drivers who just left the International Beer Drinkers Convention. Prudence might dictate in this case that you pull over and spend the night at the hotel. The obvious difference between the two situations is your perception of the likelihood of getting hurt. But this is only one part of the equation. We not only have to make a judgment as the *probability* of harm, but also a judgment as to the potential *magnitude* of the harm if it indeed occurs.

A cousin of mine kept after me to go skydiving with him. He told me that it is one of the safest activities you can do. According to the United States Parachute Association, there were only .007 fatalities per 1000 jumps in 2010. This is a lot safer statistically than say mountain climbing or scuba diving. Was I convinced? No. I agreed that the probability of injury was relatively small, but the magnitude of the injury, when it does happen is catastrophic. Thus, I made a judgment not to partake in the activity.[5]

Probability and magnitude of injury are the two moving targets in any decision that we make when it comes to risk analysis. But it does not end there. Even though we may decide that there is an increased probability of harm, and the harm may be significant, how badly do we want to do the activity? Put this in the context of employment. If I offered to pay you ten dollars an hour to take a job that we believe has both a high probability of harm, and a magnitude of harm that is significant, would you take the job? Probably not. However, instead of ten dollars an hour, how about one hundred

---

5 Years later, that same cousin was killed in a parachuting accident.

dollars? Depending on how you see the probability/magnitude equation, there may be some dollar amount that you would accept regardless of the increased perceived risk. Thus, for instance, armed security guards are usually paid more than unarmed guards. Why? Greater risk.

So does this mean that we should simply let the market determine what is a safe working environment? Most of us would say no for several reasons. First, many employees will not have a perfect understanding of the risks that a given job may entail. Put differently, you can only be asked to assume, and perhaps put a price tag on, known or reasonably foreseeable risks. This presumes that you have the information to make that assumption and, where appropriate, a pricing decision. However, it is not always realistic to make that presumption. Second, the market view also presupposes an equal bargaining position between the employer and the employee. This equality of position is seldom the case. Thus, an employee may feel that he or she really does not have a choice in taking a more dangerous job than they would otherwise like. Third, as a matter of public policy, our society has made a decision that workers have a right to be protected from foreseeable harm, at least in so far as providing information to the worker and job safety laws can do.

This last point, job safety laws, goes to the enforcement of this public policy. This role is generally under the jurisdiction of OSHA, the Occupational Safety and Health Administration of the Federal government. It is charged with developing and enforcing job safety regulations. For any regulation to be useful it must be both technologically and economically possible. It doesn't accomplish much to require a level of safety for an industry if the technology needed to reach that level does not exist or if it does, its implementation would bankrupt the industry. Over the years there has been an uneasy relationship between business and OSHA, each trying to find a balance between worker safety and this technological and economic reality. From an ethical perspective, we can't do much about the existence or non-existence of a given technology. However, as to the economic issue, many suggest that a cost-benefit analysis be the guide. That is, from a utilitarian viewpoint, are the supposed benefits of not having a regulation outweighed by the costs of implementing a new regulation. Does a given regulation cost more than the benefits received? If so, do not implement the regulation. Although attractive on its face, as the subject matter is workers' safety, is that really the best approach? How many injuries or deaths do we need to decide that the benefits of not having a regulation are now outweighed by the costs? Is worker safety simply another item subject to a market view of economics? U.S. public policy is still undecided in answering these questions. I suspect that the tension between business and regulators in the health and safety field will continue, but the momentum seems to favor workers' rights as something more than a market commodity.

7.6 DO YOU HAVE A RIGHT TO PRIVACY IN THE WORKPLACE?

If this were a Business Law book, we could answer this question easily and move on to our next topic. The general rule as to workplace privacy rights is that you don't have any. You may think that the computer you have at your job is your computer. It's not.

It's the company's computer. As such the company has the right, at any time, to see what you are doing with *their* computer. Not only does this mean that they can look at your internet browsing habits, but have a complete right to look at any of your e-mails and the like. Do you have a company cell phone? Same thing. It's not your phone, it's theirs, and the same rules apply just as if it was the company computer.

However, this is an ethics book. As such, should there be any restrictions on an employer's right to information regarding their employees? I think the answer is yes. I suggest that we break down the discussion into areas that one could reasonable say are legitimately job related, and those areas that are not.

As a general proposition it can be reasonably argued that any information that is legitimately related to your job is fair game. Let's start at the beginning, your initial application and interview for a particular job. Does your prospective employer have a right to know things such as your educational background and prior job experience? As it relates to employment, the answer is yes. Does the company have a right to know about your current marital status, sexual orientation, religious beliefs or personal hobbies? In most cases the answer is no in so far as they are not reasonably related to your prospective job. I say in most cases in that we could easily come up with some exceptions. For example, if you were applying for a job as a religion teacher for a particular religious organization, it might not be unreasonable to ask if you share the same religious beliefs as the organization for which you want to work. However, these waters can get muddy.

An employer might claim that character is a very important aspect of any employee that they may hire. As such, they should have the right to probe a job applicant as to issues concerning that applicant's character. On its face that may seem reasonable. However, "character" can be a slippery word. Attitudes and lifestyles that may appear to you, or maybe even to most people to have nothing to do with your character, your honesty or integrity, could well be interpreted differently by a prospective employer who may have certain prejudices against people with just such attitudes or lifestyles. If an employer were to believe that all Democrats were dishonest, then he could argue that asking your political affiliation goes to determining your character. Legal restrictions on job interview questions are fairly limited. In general, you are not to be asked questions about your age, race, national origin, marital or parental status, membership in the National Guard or Reserves, legal affiliations or legal product use, or disabilities.[6] Further, questions that seem innocuous but could be used to determine any of these prohibited questions are also legally suspect. Asking, "where are you from", or "was English your first language" may be really designed to determine national origin. Other than that, the interviewer has some pretty broad leeway in what they may ask.

So what are you to do? Is asking you if you are a Democrat where there is no reasonable job connection an illegal question? Probably. But there you are. The interviewer has asked the question. How do you respond? If you are comfortable giving an answer, "No, in fact I am a Republican," have at it. But what if you are not comfortable with an illegal question? Well, you have only a few choices. First, you could look surprised at the question and say something like "Gee, I've never been asked that before at a job interview." This is a gentle hint that the question you were asked was not proper. Want

---

6 This is not by any means a complete list of the dos and don'ts of legal interview questions. Rather, this is intended only as general guidelines.

to be more direct? "That question is against the law to ask," or "How is that question related to this job position?" Now there is no doubt that the last two responses are not going to make for a happy interview experience for either you or the interviewer, and you probably should not hold your breath waiting for the job offer. Although it may be illegal and unethical to discriminate against you for the reasons given above, there is no law that says the company cannot discriminate against you for the type of car you drive. In other words, the company can, and will, come up with some plausible explanation as to why they did not extend you an offer.

Note that I did not suggest what some may consider the obvious, lie. Of course we can spin this as a rationalization. That would go something like this. As the interviewer asked an illegal question, he has given up any right to receive a truthful answer. Therefore, it's all right to lie to him. As this is a rationalization, you know that this is wrong. My advice, don't do it. There is more at stake here than the job interview. When you agree to work for someone you are giving that person or company a part of your life, which you will never get back. Is this the type of company that you really want to work for, that you want to give that part of your life to? Do you seriously believe that things will be better and more ethical in the company after you get the job? I wouldn't count on it. Your best move is just that, to move on.

7.7 CHAPTER HIGHLIGHTS

1. What does the United Nations Universal Declaration of Human Rights say about a person's right to work?

The Declarations says everyone has the right to work, to free choice of employment, to just and favorable conditions of work and to protection against unemployment.

2. Between the private and public sector, which has the primary responsibility to provide a job to any individual seeking one?

Neither the private nor the public sector has a specific responsibility to provide a job to any individual seeking one.

3. What is the current policy of the United States in dealing with the unemployed?

The current policy of the U.S. is to provide for safety nets for the unemployed and others who are distressed. This takes the form of unemployment compensation, certain welfare programs and the like.

4. What does "right to work" mean in a legal context?

If you are in a so-called right to work state, you cannot be forced to join or stay in a union that may exist in your place of employment. That also means that you cannot be forced to pay union dues if you opt out of the union, nor can your employer or the union pressure or otherwise coerce you into joining the union.

5. What is the employment at will doctrine?

The doctrine of employment at will states that if there is no employment contract or law to the contrary, employers have the right to hire, promote, demote or fire any employee at any time, for any reason, including no reason.

6. What are three arguments in favor of employment at will?

First, there is the property right argument. The owner of the business is just that, the owner. It's his business, his property if you will, and he has a right to do with it as he so chooses.

Second, there is the freedom of contract argument. Both the employer and the employee have a right to negotiate any deal that they want. If you don't like an employment at will situation, part of the bargaining process between you and the employer might include a provision or agreement that exempts you from this situation.

A third argument is one based on practicality. If an employer was required to show cause, that is, give a reason when it wants to terminate an employee that the employer felt was not performing, that would result in a lengthy and time consuming process that is both costly and inefficient.

7. What are the two aspects of due process?

The first is procedural due process. What this requires is that there is some reasonable mechanism in place that an aggrieved party can look to in order to find some redress for his or her complaint.

The second aspect of due process is what we call substantive due process. In its broadest sense substantive due process means that after availing yourself of the procedural processes that are in place, you are entitled to some rational explanation and result.

8. What are the general reasonability requirements for a covenant not to compete to be enforceable?

The reasonability test means that they must be reasonable in three areas: time, territory and legitimate business interest.

9. What is a confidentiality or non-disclosure agreement?

In its simplest form, the employee agrees not to disclose to anyone, either during his employment or for a period thereafter, any confidential or proprietary information of the current employer. This information usually includes client lists, financial information, trade secrets, business plans, and confidential production techniques and just about anything else that an employer may list.

10. What are the two factors that we should consider when assessing the risk of any activity?

We have to make a judgment as the *probability* of harm, as well the potential *magnitude* of the harm if it indeed occurs.

11. How can we best characterize an employee's right to privacy regarding company computers, cell phones, e-mails and the like?

The general rule as to workplace privacy rights in the above examples is that you don't have any.

PROBLEM FOR DISCUSSION

Megacorp has decided that it must do more to safeguard the health and safety of its employees. It noted that activities that the company felt were unhealthy could cause not only injury or illness to its employees, but also an increase in the company's health care costs. So the company advised all of its employees that from now on, the following activities were prohibited, even though those activities may take place in the employees own home, and off the company property. The new rules, in part, stated as follows:

1. No employee shall be allowed to smoke cigarettes at any time or in any place. If, after a random drug test, any tobacco is found in the employee's system, the employee will be terminated.
2. As the company has decided that motorcycles are inherently dangerous to the health and well being of its employees, no employee shall ride or otherwise use a motorcycle.
3. Certain other sporting activities have also been determined to be a health risk to employees. Any employee found to have participated in snow skiing, football, or any other contact sport shall be subject to termination.
4. Any employee whose weight is more than ten pounds over company approved optimum weight levels (BMI of no more than 26) shall be given three months to lose that excess weight or be subject to termination.
5. As additional unhealthy activities and conditions are identified, employees will be so notified.

Megacorp, being in an employment at will state, feels confident that it can enforce these rules regardless of whether the "violation" took place at work, at home, or anywhere else the employee may be.

Do you think that Megacorp is within its ethical rights to promulgate these rules? If so, why, if not why not?

CHAPTER EIGHT

Diversity and Discrimination

8.1 INTRODUCTION

Slaves were first introduced in North America in the early 1600s. From that time on, the history of race relations in the New World, and subsequently the United States, has not been a pretty picture. From being considered 3/5 of a person in the original Constitution, through the Civil War, and well into current times, the issue of minorities, especially black minorities, has occupied the moral and legal consciousness of the Country as have few other issues outside of war. Business has certainly not been immune from these discussions. If you want to have a spirited, if not a downright angry debate, bring up affirmative action in hiring and promotion. There is probably no other issue in business ethics more controversial than the issue of diversity and discrimination. In this Chapter we will discuss the differing approaches to this issue as well as the arguments for and against a given position. We will conclude the Chapter by discussing the problem sexual harassment in the workplace, which is nothing more than a different sort of discrimination. As you review the material under affirmative action you will see that I have presented the material in a point-counter-point format. This is intended to give you an idea as to the complexity and the intensity of the discussions surrounding this important area of business ethics. As you read through the arguments, keep an open mind, and see where you come out on the issue.

8.2 AFFIRMATIVE ACTION

The 1950s and 1960s saw massive demonstrations and protests aimed at putting an end to discrimination and segregation against African Americans. Things came to a boiling point in 1955 in Montgomery, Alabama, when Rosa Parks, a black woman, refused to give up her seat on a bus to a white person after being ordered to do so by the bus driver. Along with the Supreme Court decision of Brown vs. the Board of Education a year earlier that outlawed segregation in public schools, the start of the great civil rights movement in the United States had begun in earnest. Finally, Congress passed the landmark Civil Rights Act of 1964 which has been the focus of the nation's attention ever since. One of the key provisions of the Act, and our focus in this Chapter, states as follows:

> **SEC. 2000e-2.** *[Section 703]*
> (a) Employer practices
>
> It shall be an unlawful employment practice for an employer -
>
> (1) to fail or refuse to hire or to discharge any individual, or otherwise to discriminate against any individual with respect to his compensation, terms, conditions, or privileges of employment, because of such individual's race, color, religion, sex, or national origin; or
>
> (2) to limit, segregate, or classify his employees or applicants for employment in any way which would deprive or tend to deprive any individual of employment opportunities or otherwise adversely affect his status as an employee, because of such individual's race, color, religion, sex, or national origin.

The obvious intent of the law was to see that minorities are afforded both equal opportunity in accessing the job market as well receiving equal treatment once they are on the job. From a business perspective, we are tempted to say the short version of this law is fairly clear: stop discriminating against people based on their race, color, religion, sex or national origin. But of course things are not that simple. To simply say "stop it" does little to nothing to make up for the history of past discrimination and the fact that due to past discriminatory policies minorities were and are still effectively blocked from gaining full and equal access to the job market. Simply saying that from now on, business won't discriminate anymore may not be enough. Presuming that this is true, that discrimination in business does in fact still persist, what more can or should business do beyond simply saying "stop it" to end this injustice? How we answer this question will determine how we view affirmative action programs.

Before we look at the arguments for and against these programs let's first agree on a definition. The U.S. Commission of Civil Rights offers the following definition which is as good as any. Affirmative action is "any measure...that permits the consideration of race, national origin, sex or disability, along with other criteria, and which is adopted to provide opportunities to a class of qualified individuals who have either historically or actually been denied those opportunities and/or to prevent the recurrence of discrimination in the future."[1] The first thing that we can take away from this definition is that affirmative action is something more than just passive nondiscrimination. That's the "just stop it" concept mentioned above. Instead, affirmative action is something more. It is where a company takes specific and definitive steps to hire or promote from groups that have either historically been discriminated against or are presently discriminated against. These steps can range from as little as target advertising for minorities to specific hiring preferences up to and including outright hiring quotas. For our purposes here, we will look at the most controversial of affirmative action programs, hiring preferences.

8.3 PREFERENTIAL HIRING

A preference in hiring or promoting someone is just what it sounds like. It is where you prefer one candidate over another. In itself, there is nothing wrong with this. We prefer, discriminate if you will, between things and people all the time. The fact that we make discriminations, judgments, in itself is not very interesting. Where the issue gets complicated is when we ask ourselves why we have a certain preference. That "why" may be either rational or irrational. Let's say that you own a construction company. It's now time to buy a new vehicle for your business. You carry around a lot of tools and building materials. The car salesman says that what you really need this new Honda Civic. Based on your needs, you may come to the rational decision that a pick-up truck is far more suited to your needs. You can articulate the reason, and the odds are good that few would disagree with your decision. It is purely rational. But sometimes we make other decisions that do not seem so rational. We have all met the person that on first meeting, however brief, we conclude we really don't like this person. If asked why, we may be hard pressed to give a reason. The best we can do may be something along the lines of "I don't know. I just don't like him." This does not mean that the person in question is in fact a bad person. We admit that we don't really know that. But nevertheless we have this feeling. This is not rational. It is nothing more than a feeling, sometimes a bare emotion. However, we oftentimes act solely based on those feelings and emotions, and oftentimes they turn out to be right. So we make decisions about people and things from both the rational and the irrational sides of our being. The same is true when we look at hiring someone.

Your company needs to expand its accounting department. You interview three applicants for the job of staff accountant. The first applicant has a degree in history, and does a great job explaining the historical development of the wheel. The second applicant has a degree in accounting with an outstanding academic background. In fact, he graduated first in his class. You notice, however, that he has not seemed to have taken a shower in a few weeks and showed up for the interview wearing jeans and a T shirt and seemed totally lacking in interpersonal skills. The third candidate has a degree in accounting with acceptable, but not outstanding academic skills in the field. However, he dresses (and smells) appropriately for the interview and scored high on the "likeability scale." Who will you hire? You will probably immediately dismiss the

---

1 U.S. Commission on Civil Rights, Office of the General Counsel, Briefing Paper for the U.S. Commission on Civil Rights: Legislative, Executive and Judicial Development of Affirmative Action, Washington, D.C., Mar. 1995.

first applicant because he is unqualified for the job. Few would disagree. Certain jobs have bona fide job qualifications without which you cannot expect to be hired. What about candidate number two? If the only criterion for hiring was academic ability in his field, he would get the job. Arguably this is the most rational decision you could make. But how many would actually hire this person? Probably very few. The third candidate, although not as technically qualified as the second, will probably get the job if for no other reason than you liked him. Perhaps both rational and irrational aspects of our personality come into play when making these types of decisions. Is there anything ethically wrong with this decision making process? Usually not. We get into trouble, however, when we base these decisions on factors that have nothing whatsoever to do with the job in question.

In the above example, how many of us would say that it is an ethically defensible position to hire candidate three over candidate two if the primary reason for hiring number three was that you liked him more than two? Now take it a step further. What if it turned out that candidate number two in fact did not have the personal hygiene and interpersonal challenges claimed by the interviewer? What if in fact, the only thing that distinguished him from number three was that he was a minority? What if the primary reason that number three was hired, or more honestly, number two was not hired, was because of number two's race, color, religion, sex, or national origin? How many would consider this to be ethically justified? None of these traits have anything to do with the job in question. More so, as we saw above, to engage in this type of hiring practice violates the law. But of course this goes beyond the law. To discriminate against others based solely on irrational reasons that by definition have nothing to do with the job denies the affected person their human dignity. This is never ethically defensible.

So what does business do about this? As we talked about above, just saying "stop it" is not enough. Why? Say that you were the person who was denied a job solely because of your race. Would you be content to be told not to worry about it because the business will not do this again to the next applicant? I suspect not. You might very well say "what about me?" You have been done a wrong, you have been harmed. Is simply saying, sorry, I won't do it again, enough for you? Probably not. And that is where the situation gets complicated. What about all of those others who are and have in the past been treated this way? Are they entitled to receive compensation for those harms? If so, how do we do that? That is where affirmative action comes in.

Preference hiring in affirmative action is most often justified as a form of compensatory justice. The concept is that if someone has done some harm to you, you have a right to be compensated for the harmed caused. If someone goes through a red light and hits you in your car and you are injured, you have a right to be compensated for your injuries caused by that other driver. In like manner, if you have been wrongfully discriminated against in the job market, you should have a right to be compensated for the harm suffered. More so, no one denies that discriminatory practices have gone on for literally centuries. Does not justice demand that some form of compensation be provided to make up for those past harms? Although this may seem reasonable on its face, opponents of this compensatory justice argument make the following points.

First, and going back to our car accident example, the person required to pay the money should be the person who caused the harm. There appears no argument from justice that says if Jones is the one who caused the harm, that Smith, who had nothing to do with the accident, is the fellow who should pay for the damages. Jones did it, Jones is the one who has to pay. Second, the person receiving the compensation for the harm should be the person who in fact suffered the harm. Jones hits your car. But instead of you receiving the compensation for your damages, we give the money to Smith, who again had nothing to do with any of this. From the perspective of affirmative action programs, the same two arguments are raised.

First, typically these programs are designed to benefit a particular group. And this benefit is provided, "paid" if you will, to members of that group regardless of the fact they individually may or may not have ever been discriminated against. In fact, so the argument goes, the compensation being paid may be based on harms done to people who have long since died. Second, even if you could show that this particular member of the group has in fact been discriminated against, simply stated "I" am not the one that caused the harm, that engaged in the discrimination. So why should "I" be required to pay for the harm done by someone else? Note that the "I" of which I speak is the non-minority who feels that he or she was not hired because a hiring preference based solely on race, for example, was used to give the job to someone else. In this case, the non-minority may ask where is the justice in this?

What is the response to this? First, our history shows that discrimination has not been on an individual event basis. Rather, women and minorities have been discriminated against in education and employment throughout the larger part of our history. It has been both systemic and systematic for quite literally a few centuries. To believe that such discrimination somehow came to a screeching halt with the passage of the Civil Rights Act of 1964 is patently untrue. It is the result of this past discrimination that minorities to this day still do not have equal access to education and jobs. Thus there is a continuing harm being done, and justice requires that action be taken to remedy that harm. Does that mean that there will be some minorities who perhaps have never experienced any discrimination that will benefit from certain affirmative action and preferential hiring programs? Yes, it does. Does that also mean that there may be some non-minorities who will suffer a personal injustice by being excluded from a particular job or educational opportunity because of these programs? Yes it does as well. But that is a small price to pay for the overall ending of discrimination in this country.

A second argument given by proponents of affirmative action and preferential hiring programs is based on what some call the distributive justice argument. The concept is that the benefits and burdens of society should be shared equally by all of its citizens. In order to receive some of the benefits of American society, a good education, a good job and the like, almost by definition implies that you are given the opportunity to take advantage of those benefits. The history of discrimination in our society shows that minorities and women have systematically been excluded from those opportunities. The simplest example perhaps is education. Presume that a college degree is needed to land a great many high paying jobs. If you were told that because of your race, you could not be admitted to college, does this not in fact deny you the opportunity to ever get one of those jobs? Of course it does. Thus various affirmative action programs do nothing more than level the playing field. They provide opportunities to share in society's benefits that would otherwise simply not be available to these affected groups.

The counter position to this argument is that it wrongfully focuses only on benefits. In its haste to assure that everyone has an equal opportunity to share in society's benefits it unjustly shifts society's burdens to its non-affected members, especially white males. They would argue that in the present time, as a group they had nothing to do with either past or current discrimination, and should not be required to take upon itself the burden of rectifying discrimination that they neither caused nor participated in. Even granting the fact that there was and is discrimination, it is argued that it is wrong to try and remedy one injustice by committing another.

In response to this objection, it is argued that for present day white males to say that they have not benefited, or are not beneficiaries of past discrimination policies is simply not true. The reason that they have the present opportunities to better jobs and an education is due, at least in part, to the systematic denial of those same opportunities to minorities and women in the past. Thus again, these programs are simply leveling the playing field.

Last, those opposed to affirmative action and preferential hiring programs argue that regardless of concepts such as compensatory and distributive justice, these programs do not really work. In fact, they cause more harm to society than good. They advance at least three arguments to this point.

First look at this from the company perspective. Let's go back to our example of your company wanting to hire an accountant. If you were the boss, and your manager came to you and said he has three candidates, what criteria should he used in deciding which one to hire, I suspect that most of us would say, "the most qualified." Seems simple enough. But what if you have a preferential hiring program in effect? This could mean, (although not necessarily) that you would give the job to a less qualified minority. As a result, the quality of your workforce is lower than you would otherwise have or desire.

Next, let's look at this from the standpoint of the minority. Although it was never part of the official language of business, everyone knew what it meant to be "an affirmative action hire." It was understood that this meant that the employee was somehow less competent and worthy of the job or promotion than other non-minority applicants. Whether this was true or not did not matter. This label, this stigma stayed with the employee throughout their career, oftentimes regardless of how successful they were in the given job position. More so, these programs create an environment of dependency by the minority. If an individual believes that they will get preferential treatment based solely on their minority status, this acts as a disincentive for that person to work hard and advance solely on their own merits. As a result, the program giving them a preference really harmed them more than helped.

The last argument is probably the most powerful. If a large segment of society, white males, feel that the deck is stacked against them, that no matter how hard they work or what their accomplishments may be, they will lose out of an educational or job opportunity to a perceived less qualified minority, the results can be severe. This will create resentment if not downright anger increasing, not lessening the tensions and animosities that may already exist between the races. Although it might be said that this is nothing more or different from what minorities have suffered from for decades, if the goal is to lessen racial tensions, preference hiring is not a good approach. Further, it appears that the law is moving towards this position as well. In fact we have seen many so called "reverse discrimination" lawsuits claiming that any race based hiring is simply wrong and unconstitutional. (In a recent Supreme Court case, Chief Justice John Roberts stated that, "The way to stop discrimination based on race is to stop discriminating based on race."[2] Although this case involved an educational setting, it is being argued that any race based program may no longer be legally permissible.)

As you may have guessed by now, each of the above arguments, against these programs, have counter positions. Have these programs really resulted in less qualified, and therefore by implication, under-performing employees? There is no evidence to support this. As for stigmatizing the minority, the counter to that argument is that even if true, if you asked the employee in question whether he or she would rather be out of a job completely or put up with perceived stigmatization, I suspect most would opt for the job as the lesser of two evils. As for the final argument, that these programs create more racial tension, once again, proponents of the programs are willing to accept that as a fair trade off to remedy a greater injustice. And for the overall position that these programs harm society more than help, again, there is no evidence to support that position. In fact, we might draw some contrary conclusions. For example, if people who are otherwise disadvantaged are now employed, this not only raises their individual situation to a higher level, but also helps to reduce poverty and crime, lessens dependence on government, provides role models for others who are disadvantaged and from there provides many other additional societal benefits.

So what are we do make of all of this? Is there no common ground between those favoring preferential hiring programs and those in opposition? At least to some extent, I believe that there is. First, when it comes to job qualifications as the primary emphasis in the hiring decision making process, most would agree that where one job candidate is clearly more qualified for the position than another, the benefit of the doubt should go the more qualified. I say "benefit of the doubt" in that this is true for some positions more than others. For example, the company is looking to hire an accountant to handle relatively simple accounts receivable and payable. The minority candidate has a bachelor's degree in accounting. The non-minority candidate has a Ph.D. in accounting. Does this mean that the non-minority should be given the job? Not necessarily. The job in question does not require the qualifications of a PhD. Thus the minority candidate's qualifications should be considered just as acceptable as the non-minority based on the specific job in question. It is fine and good for a company to establish job qualifications. However, those qualifications must be reasonable, not arbitrary, and applied uniformly. More so, many would agree that a diverse workforce provides benefits to a company that a strictly homogenous work force does not. Management often will benefit from different views of an issue that only a diverse workforce will provide.

Second, most would agree that at a minimum, everyone should be afforded equal opportunity in both employment and education, at least as far as their abilities will take them. Any hiring policy that stacks the deck against minorities solely because they are minorities or bases hiring decisions on factors that are not related to the job in

2 Parents Involved in Community Schools v. Seattle School District No. 1, 551 U.S. 701 (2007)

question is unjust and unethical. Does this mean that a company should not go beyond passive non-discrimination? As we discussed above, that argument still rages.

As I said at the beginning of this Chapter, affirmative action and preferential hiring policies are some of the most contentious issues in business today. As you may have gathered from the above discussions, the arguments in favor of such programs and the arguments in opposition are significant. From a legal perspective, the United States Supreme Court may very well settle some of these arguments, at least as a matter of law. However, regardless of any Court decision, the ethical arguments are certainly going to continue.

8.4 SEXUAL HARASSMENT

Another area of contention in business today concerns itself with claims of sexual harassment. It is important that you have a good understanding of what sexual harassment is not only to obviously avoid being guilty of such a thing, but also to recognize it when you may experience it as a victim. The first place to start in understanding exactly what constitutes sexual harassment is the United States Equal Employment Opportunity Commission. Here is what it says.

> Sexual harassment is a form of sex discrimination that violates Title VII of the Civil Rights Act of 1964.
>
> Unwelcome sexual advances, requests for sexual favors, and other verbal or physical conduct of a sexual nature constitutes sexual harassment when submission to or rejection of this conduct explicitly or implicitly affects an individual's employment, unreasonably interferes with an individual's work performance or creates an intimidating, hostile or offensive work environment.
>
> Sexual harassment can occur in a variety of circumstances, including but not limited to the following:
> - The victim as well as the harasser may be a woman or a man. The victim does not have to be of the opposite sex.
> - The harasser can be the victim's supervisor, an agent of the employer, a supervisor in another area, a co-worker, or a non-employee.
> - The victim does not have to be the person harassed but could be anyone affected by the offensive conduct.
> - Unlawful sexual harassment may occur without economic injury to or discharge of the victim.
> - The harasser's conduct must be unwelcome.[3]

To understand where the EEOC gets this, and how this applies in the workplace, consider the case of Meritor Savings Bank vs. Vinson, which set the standard in understanding the rules governing sexual harassment.[4]

---

3 The U.S. Equal Employment Opportunity Commission, Facts About Sexual Harassment
4 Meritor Savings Bank v. Vinson - 477 U.S. 57 (1986)

In 1974, Mechelle Vinson met Sidney Taylor, a vice-president of Meritor Savings Bank and manager of one of its branch offices. When she asked whether she might obtain employment at the bank, Taylor gave her an application, which she completed and returned the next day. Later that same day, Taylor called her to say that she had been hired. With Taylor as her supervisor, Mechelle started as a teller-trainee, and thereafter was promoted to teller, head teller, and assistant branch manager. She worked at the same branch for four years, and her advancement there was based on merit alone. In September, 1978, she notified Taylor that she was taking sick leave for an indefinite period. On November 1, 1978, the bank discharged her for excessive use of that leave. At least that was the Bank's story. Mechelle had a very different one.

She filed a lawsuit against Taylor and the bank, claiming that, during her four years at the bank, she had "constantly been subjected to sexual harassment" by Taylor in violation of Title VII. She testified that, during her probationary period as a teller-trainee, Taylor treated her in a fatherly way and made no sexual advances. Shortly thereafter, however, he invited her out to dinner and, during the course of the meal, suggested that they go to a motel to have sexual relations. At first she refused, but out of what she described as fear of losing her job, she eventually agreed. According to her, Taylor thereafter made repeated demands upon her for sexual favors, usually at the branch, both during and after business hours; she estimated that over the next several years she had intercourse with him some 40 or 50 times. In addition, she testified that Taylor fondled her in front of other employees, followed her into the women's restroom when she went there alone, exposed himself to her, and even forcibly raped her on several occasions. Finally, she admitted that because she was afraid of Taylor, she never reported his harassment to any of his supervisors and never attempted to use the bank's complaint procedure. Taylor's side of the story was that none of this ever happened, or if it did happen, Mechelle had voluntarily consented to the relationship.

Apparently no one really thought that the allegations in Mechelle's complaint against Taylor weren't true. They probably were. The real question came down to this: if the actions that Mechelle were complaining about were voluntarily entered into by Mechelle, could she claim sexual harassment? Here is what the Court said, and this has become the standard for understanding what constitutes sexual harassment ever since.

There are two types of sexual harassment situations. The first is called "quid pro quo." This is the easiest one to identify. This occurs when someone, usually in authority over the employee, demands sexual favors in return for some job benefit. This could be in getting the job itself, a pay raise or promotion, or even as a condition of keeping their current job. Most of the time you will know this type of harassment when you see it. The second type of harassment is not always so easy to identify, This is called the creation of "an offensive or hostile work environment." Where a quid pro case affects some concrete work and economic benefit, the second, the hostile work environment does not. This occurs where "such conduct has the purpose or effect of unreasonably interfering with an individual's work performance or creating an intimidating, hostile, or offensive working environment." Over the years, a lot of these somewhat vague terms such as "unreasonably interfering" or "intimidating" have been better defined.

Under current EEOC Guidelines, and taken from the Vinson case, in order for there to be liability for creating a hostile work environment, you have to show the following.[5]

1. The conduct in question must be unwelcome. This is most often the greatest area of contention between the parties so let's spend some time with this. Generally this means that the employee did not solicit or incite it, and that the employee regarded the conduct as undesirable or offensive. And, as the Court in Vinson pointed out, because an employee may agree to participate in some conduct, that in itself does not mean that it is welcome. In other words the employee may consent out of fear of losing her job or suffering some other penalty. An employee's claim that the conduct was unwelcome obviously is strengthened if she makes it clear to the other person that she does not appreciate what he is doing and/or reports the unwelcome conduct to her supervisor or other company officials.

However, courts have also said they could consider whether the complainant welcomed the sexual conduct by acting in a sexually aggressive manner herself, using sexually-oriented language, or soliciting the sexual conduct. Thus, in one case, the lady in question regularly used vulgar language, initiated sexually-oriented conversations with her co-workers, asked male employees about their marital sex lives and whether they engaged in extramarital affairs, and discussed her own sexual encounters. In rejecting her claim of "hostile environment" harassment, the court found that any propositions or sexual remarks by co-workers were "prompted by her own sexual aggressiveness and her own sexually-explicit conversations."[6]

2. The conduct in question must be based on sex. Thus, for instance, simply because you may have an unreasonably demanding boss does not make his work demand rise to the level of sexual harassment.

3. The conduct in question must be sufficiently severe or pervasive to alter the conditions of the victim's employment and create an abusive working environment. Thus, not every off color comment rises to the level of sexual harassment. Or in the words of one court, Title VII does not serve "as a vehicle for vindicating the petty slights suffered by the hypersensitive."[7] If the challenged conduct would not substantially affect the work environment of a reasonable person, no violation should be found. And this leads us to our last element.

4. Whether the actions being complained of are unwelcome, based on sex, and severe or pervasive are to be judged under the "reasonable person" standard. This means that we are not going to judge these issues by only going with what the complaining person said. Rather, we ask whether a reasonable person, under the same circumstances would also feel that the actions in question were unwelcome, sex based and severe. That of course is ultimately what a court may have to decide.

What types of behavior could be considered sexual harassment? Well, as has been said, not every individual comment is actionable, but obvious things to avoid would include:

---

5 U.S. Equal Employment Opportunity Commission, Policy Guidance on Current Issues of Sexual Harassment.
6 Gan v. Kepro Circuit Systems, 27 EPD ¶ 32,379 (E.D. Mo. 1982)
7 Zabkowicz v. West Bend Co., 589 F. Supp. 780, 784, 35 EPD ¶ 34, 766 (E.D. Wis. 1984).

- Sexual pranks, or repeated sexual teasing, jokes, or innuendo, in person or via e-mail;
- Verbal abuse of a sexual nature;
- Touching or grabbing of a sexual nature;
- Repeatedly standing too close to or brushing up against a person;
- Repeatedly asking a person to socialize during off-duty hours when the person has said no or has indicated he or she is not interested (supervisors in particular should be careful not to pressure their employees to socialize);
- Giving gifts or leaving objects that are sexually suggestive;
- Repeatedly making sexually suggestive gestures;
- Making or posting sexually demeaning or offensive pictures, cartoons or other materials in the workplace;
- Off-duty, unwelcome conduct of a sexual nature that affects the work environment.[8]
- Sexually-oriented offensive names;
- Sexually suggestive sounds or gestures;

This list does not include everything that could be construed as conduct of a sexually harassing nature. When in doubt, use the mom or grandma test. Would you say or do the action in question with mom or grandma? If not, you probably should not do it with or to a co-worker.

From the perspective of the company, what should it do to prevent sexual harassment in its workplace? Again, the EEOC gives us some fairly good guidelines. The company should have an effective preventive program which:

1. Should include an explicit policy against sexual harassment that is clearly and regularly communicated to employees and effectively implemented.
2. The employer should affirmatively raise the subject with all supervisory and non-supervisory employees, express strong disapproval, and explain the sanctions for harassment.
3. The employer should also have a procedure for resolving sexual harassment complaints. The procedure should be designed to "encourage victims of harassment to come forward" and should not require a victim to complain first to the offending supervisor who often may be the source of the harassment. It should ensure confidentiality as much as possible and provide effective remedies, including protection of victims and witnesses against retaliation."[9]

What should the company do after it receives a complaint?

1. When an employer receives a complaint or otherwise learns of alleged sexual harassment in the workplace, the employer should investigate promptly and thoroughly.

---

8   United States Department of State, Policy on Sexual Harassment.
9   IBID

2. The employer should take immediate and appropriate corrective action by doing whatever is necessary to end the harassment.

3. The employer should make the victim whole by restoring lost employment benefits or opportunities, and prevent the misconduct from recurring.

4. The employer should take disciplinary action against the offending supervisor or employee, ranging from reprimand to discharge. Generally, the corrective action should reflect the severity of the conduct.

5. The employer should make follow-up inquiries to ensure the harassment has not resumed and the victim has not suffered retaliation."[10]

Sexual harassment is wrong, both legally and morally. It robs an individual of their human dignity and as Kant would put it, makes the other nothing more than an object for someone else's amusement or personal gain. It also comes with a cost to the company, and not just in terms of legal liability. Victims of sexual harassment, although oftentimes very good employees, are less likely to stay with a company where this type of conduct is tolerated. Employee morale, an intangible but very real asset of a company also suffers greatly in these types of hostile environments. Simply put, nothing good ever comes out of this type of conduct.

8.5 CHAPTER HIGHLIGHTS

1. What are the key provisions of the Civil Rights Act of 1964 regarding discrimination in the workplace?

It shall be an unlawful employment practice for an employer -

(1) to fail or refuse to hire or to discharge any individual, or otherwise to discriminate against any individual with respect to his compensation, terms, conditions, or privileges of employment, because of such individual's race, color, religion, sex, or national origin; or

(2) to limit, segregate, or classify his employees or applicants for employment in any way which would deprive or tend to deprive any individual of employment opportunities or otherwise adversely affect his status as an employee, because of such individual's race, color, religion, sex, or national origin.

2. How does the U.S. Commission of Civil Rights define affirmative action?

Affirmative action is "any measure...that permits the consideration of race, national origin, sex or disability, along with other criteria, and which is adopted to provide opportunities to a class of qualified individuals who have either historically or actually been denied those opportunities and/or to prevent the recurrence of discrimination in the future".

3. What is meant by compensatory justice as it applies to hiring preferences?

If someone has done some harm to you, you have a right to be compensated for the harmed caused. If you have been wrongfully discriminated against in the job market, you should have a right to be compensated for the harm suffered. More so, no one

---

denies that discriminatory practices have gone on for literally centuries and as such justice demands that some form of compensation be provided to make up for those past harms.

4. What is an argument against compensatory justice in preferential hiring?

Non-minorities argue that they did not cause the harm being complained of and the recipients of the benefit did not suffer the harm for which compensation is being given.

5. What is meant by distributive justice as it applies to hiring preferences?

Benefits and burdens of society should be shared equally by all of its citizens. To receive some of the benefits of American society, you must have the opportunity to take advantage of those benefits. The history of discrimination in our society shows that minorities and women have systematically been excluded from those opportunities. Hiring preferences better distribute these opportunities and therefore these benefits.

6. What is an argument against distributive justice in preferential hiring?

The argument wrongfully focuses only on benefits. It unjustly shifts society's burdens to its non-affected members, especially white males.

7. How does the EEOC define sexual harassment?

Unwelcome sexual advances, requests for sexual favors, and other verbal or physical conduct of a sexual nature constitutes sexual harassment when submission to or rejection of this conduct explicitly or implicitly affects an individual's employment, unreasonably interferes with an individual's work performance or creates an intimidating, hostile or offensive work environment.

8. What are the two forms of sexual harassment?

The two forms of sexual harassment are the quid pro quo proposition and the creating of an offensive or hostile work environment.

9. What are the requirements for a claim of sexual harassment based on a hostile work environment?

The conduct must be unwelcome, based on sex, and severe or pervasive, all of which are to be judged under the reasonable person standard.

10. What steps should a company take to prevent sexual harassment in its workplace?

It should have an effective prevention program that among other things should include an explicit policy against sexual harassment, explain the sanctions for harassment, and have a procedure for resolving sexual harassment complaints.

11. What should the company do after it receives a complaint?

The employer should investigate promptly and thoroughly and take immediate and appropriate corrective action by doing whatever is necessary to end the harassment, make the victim whole by restoring lost employment benefits or opportunities, and prevent the misconduct from recurring. Generally, the corrective action should reflect the severity of the conduct. The employer should make follow-up inquiries to ensure the harassment has not resumed and the victim has not suffered retaliation.

PROBLEM FOR DISCUSSION

In 2003, 118 New Haven firefighters took examinations to qualify for promotion to the rank of lieutenant or captain. Promotion examinations in New Haven were infrequent, so the stakes were high. The results would determine which firefighters would be considered for promotions during the next two years, and the order in which they would be considered. Many firefighters studied for months, at considerable personal and financial cost. Here were the exam results.

Seventy-seven candidates completed the lieutenant examination—43 whites, 19 blacks, and 15 Hispanics. Of those, 34 candidates passed—25 whites, 6 blacks, and 3 Hispanics.

Forty-one candidates completed the captain examination—25 Whites, 8 Blacks, and 8 Hispanics. Of those, 22 candidates passed—16 Whites, 3 Blacks, and 3 Hispanics.

When the examination results showed that white candidates had outperformed minority candidates, the mayor and other local politicians opened a public debate that turned rancorous. Some firefighters argued the tests should be discarded because the results showed the tests to be discriminatory. They threatened a discrimination lawsuit if the City made promotions based on the tests. Other firefighters said the exams were neutral and fair. And they, in turn, threatened a discrimination lawsuit if the City ignored the test results and denied promotions to the candidates who had performed well. In the end the City took the side of those who protested the test results. It threw out the examinations. The City argued if it followed the test results that would have a disparate impact on the minority candidates. (Disparate-treatment claims present the traditional case of intentional discrimination. Disparate-impact claims attack a neutral policy or practice that has a disproportionately negative impact on the basis of race, gender, or some other statutorily-protected characteristic.)

Certain white and Hispanic firefighters who likely would have been promoted based on their good test performance sued the City saying that the City discriminated against them based on their race, in violation of Title VII of the Civil Rights Act of 1964.

- What ethical issues do you see in this case?
- What arguments would you make for the white firefighters?
- What arguments would you make for the minority firefighters?

CHAPTER NINE

Ethics in a Global Environment

9.1 INTRODUCTION

The simple fact of the matter is that we live in a global environment. If you are not sure of that just take a look at the goods and products that are in your pocket, home or driveway. A very large percentage of those are manufactured outside of the United States. Everything from the price of the oil that heats our homes and runs our cars to the clothes on our backs are all affected by events around the world. The once relatively small group of companies that called themselves "multi-national corporations" now includes virtually every member of the Fortune 500 family of companies, and a good many thousands more. The odds are excellent that most of you sooner or later are going to be involved in some aspect of international trade and business. From the perspective of business ethics, operating in other countries and dealing with other cultures can pose some significant problems for American business managers. In this chapter we are going to take a look at the most common ethical challenge faced by companies and individuals working in a global environment: bribery. As a practical matter, bribe cases in an international context come in two varieties. The first are instances where there is an attempt by a U.S. company or person to bribe a foreign official to obtain or keep business. The second deals with cases of inter-company bribery. That is where a U.S.

company bribes a foreign company in order to get that foreign company's business. First, let's look at bribes offered to foreign public officials.

9.2 BRIBERY OF FOREIGN OFFICIALS

In its broadest sense, a bribe takes place when someone offers money or some other benefit to another to influence that other person to do or not do something, usually of an illegal or dishonest nature. You may be thinking, well this is easy. You are opposed to bribery and you would never do such a thing. But are you really so sure? Here is a case that I give my students in Ethics. You are driving down the highway in a foreign country. The speed limit is sixty miles per hour. You are going fifty-five. You look in the rear view mirror and see that a police car has it lights on and is motioning to you to pull over. You quickly check your speed again, and yes, it's fifty-five. It can't be for you, you think, but you pull over anyway. The policeman stops behind you, gets out of his car, comes up to you and says that you were doing seventy miles per hour in a sixty mile per hour speed zone. Were you really speeding? No, you were not. Does the officer believe that you were speeding? No, he doesn't either, but nevertheless, there you are. The officer then says that you have a choice. You can either pay him twenty dollars on the spot and this unfortunate incident will be over, or, he will have to give you a ticket and take you to the nearest town fifty miles away for a hearing before the judge who, by the way, will not be back in town for three days and is the brother in law of the officer. All right. It's honesty time. Would you pay the twenty dollars? Would your decision be any different if in fact you were speeding and again, the officer offers to make this go away for twenty dollars? When I asked these questions to students in my Ethics course the response, after a moment of silence, is that, yes, they would pay the twenty dollars, and no, it would not matter whether they were speeding or not. These are also the same students who a moment ago said they would never pay a bribe. When I pointed out this inconsistency to the class, one student gave the following response. "To be ethical doesn't mean you have to be stupid, does it?" No, it does not.

Now let's kick the problem up a notch. Say that your company is bidding on building a bridge in a foreign country. You are not the only bidder, and in fact the competition is fierce as the profits will be in the millions of dollars. The government official in charge of making the decision as to who is to get the contract lets you know that he may look more favorably on your bid if you deposit $250,000 in his secret Swiss bank account. You also know that your other competitors, foreign corporations, are also making various payments in hopes of getting this official to give them the bid. Simply put, if you do not make the payment you are not going to get the contract. Do you make the payment?

On one level there really is no difference between our two hypothetical situations. In both cases you are effectively bribing a foreign official. However, at least for most of us, the similarity ends there. Clearly in the second case the stakes are much higher. And it is to the second case in particular that we now turn our attention.

9.3 THE FOREIGN CORRUPT PRACTICES ACT

Congress enacted the U.S. Foreign Corrupt Practices Act, or FCPA, in 1977 in response to revelations of widespread bribery of foreign officials by U.S. companies. The Act was intended to halt those corrupt practices, create a level playing field for honest businesses, and restore public confidence in the integrity of the marketplace. In the words of the House of Representatives:

> The payment of bribes to influence the acts or decisions of foreign officials, foreign political parties or candidates for foreign political office is unethical. It is counter to the moral expectations and values of the American public. But not only is it unethical, it is bad business as well. It erodes public confidence in the integrity of the free market system. It short-circuits the marketplace by directing business to those companies too inefficient to compete in terms of price, quality or service, or too lazy to engage in honest salesmanship, or too intent upon unloading marginal products. In short, it rewards corruption instead of efficiency and puts pressure on ethical enterprises to lower their standards or risk losing business.[1]

One of the benefits of a good book on ethics is that it should also help keep its readers out of jail. With that goal in mind, we are going to spend a few minutes talking about the law. As many of you will be dealing in an international environment, it is only a matter of time before you will be confronted with this issue.

So to begin with, what does the FCPA prohibit? In general, the FCPA prohibits offering to pay, paying, promising to pay, or authorizing the payment of money or anything of value to a foreign official in order to influence any act or decision of that foreign official in his or her official capacity, or to secure any other improper advantage in order to obtain or retain business. Over the years the U.S. Department of Justice has been going after a growing number of companies it believes have violated the Act. It is important that you know the general overview of the FCPA and what the government must show in order to hold either you, your company or both liable for violating it. Before the government can successfully prosecute someone for violation of the Act, its case has to pass five tests.

First, there is the question of jurisdiction, or if you will, that is, are you or your company even subject to the Act? As you will see, this is the easiest element for the government to prove in that almost everyone and every business organization may be subject to this law. Specifically, the FCPA's anti-bribery provisions apply broadly to three categories of persons and entities: (1) "issuers" and their officers, directors, employees, agents, and shareholders; (2) "domestic concerns" and their officers, directors, employees, agents, and shareholders; and (3) certain persons and entities, other than issuers and domestic concerns, acting while in the territory of the United States. An "issuer" is any company that trades its securities on a national exchange in the United States, or is traded in the over-the-counter market and required to file periodic

---

1 H.R. Rep. No. 95-640, at 4-5 (1977), available at http://www.justice.gov/criminal/fraud/fcpa/history/1977/houseprt-95-640.pdf.

reports with U.S. Securities and Exchange Commission. A company thus need not be a U.S. company to be an issuer. Foreign companies with American Depository Receipts that are listed on a U.S. exchange are also issuers.[2]

What is a domestic concern? Just about any business enterprise you can think of. Specifically under the Act, "A domestic concern is any individual who is a citizen, national, or resident of the United States, or any corporation, partnership, association, joint-stock company, business trust, unincorporated organization, or sole proprietorship that is organized under the laws of the United States or its states, territories, possessions, or commonwealths or that has its principal place of business in the United States. Officers, directors, employees, agents, or stockholders acting on behalf of a domestic concern, including foreign nationals or companies, are also covered."[3]

Last, you cannot get around the law by hiring foreign nationals to do the deed. Since 1998, the FCPA's anti-bribery provisions have applied to foreign persons and foreign entities that either directly or through an agent, "engage in any act in furtherance of a corrupt payment (or an offer, promise, or authorization to pay) while in the territory of the United States. Also, officers, directors, employees, agents, or stockholders acting on behalf of such persons or entities may be subject to the FCPA's anti-bribery prohibitions."[4] So like I suggested above, just about anyone you deal with will probably be subject to the jurisdiction of the FCPA.

The second test after who is covered is what is covered. The FCPA applies only to payments intended to induce or influence a foreign official to use his or her position "in order to assist ... in obtaining or retaining business for or with, or directing business to, any person." This requirement is known as the "business purpose test" and is broadly interpreted. Not surprisingly, many enforcement actions involve bribes to obtain or retain government contracts. The FCPA also prohibits bribes in the conduct of business or to gain a business advantage. For example, bribe payments made to secure favorable tax treatment, to reduce or eliminate customs duties, to obtain government action to prevent competitors from entering a market, or to circumvent a licensing or permit requirement, all satisfy the business purpose test.[5]

The third test is called the corrupt intent test. To violate the FCPA, an offer, promise, or authorization of a payment, or a payment, to a government official must be made "corruptly." The word "corruptly" is used to make clear that the offer, payment, promise, or gift, must be intended to induce the recipient to misuse his official position; for example, wrongfully to direct business to the payor or his client, to obtain preferential legislation or regulations, or to induce a foreign official to fail to perform an official function. By focusing on intent, the FCPA does not require that a corrupt act succeed in its purpose. Nor must the foreign official actually solicit, accept, or receive the corrupt payment for the bribe payor to be liable. For example, in one case, a specialty chemical company promised Iraqi government officials approximately $850,000 in bribes for an upcoming contract. Although the company did not, in the end, make

2 A RESOURCE GUIDE TO THE U.S. FOREIGN CORRUPT PRACTICES ACT By the Criminal Division of the U.S. Department of Justice and the Enforcement Division of the U.S. Securities and Exchange Commission, 2012 pp 10-11
3 IBID
4 IBID
5 IBID p. 13

the payment (the scheme was thwarted by the U.S. government's investigation), the company still violated the FCPA and was held accountable.[6]

The fourth test is the payment test. In enacting the FCPA, Congress recognized that bribes can come in many shapes and sizes—a broad range of unfair benefits—and so the statute prohibits the corrupt "offer, payment, promise to pay, or authorization of the payment of any money, or offer, gift, promise to give, or authorization of the giving of anything of value to" a foreign official. An improper benefit can take many forms. While cases often involve payments of cash sometimes in the guise of "consulting fees" or "commissions" given through intermediaries, others have involved travel expenses and expensive gifts. The FCPA does not contain a minimum threshold amount for corrupt gifts or payments. Indeed, what might be considered a modest payment in the United States could be a larger and much more significant amount in a foreign country. On this point we should also understand that the Act does not prohibit all forms of gift giving. A small gift or token of esteem or gratitude is often an appropriate way for business people to display respect for each other. Some indications of appropriate gift giving are when the gift is given openly and transparently, properly recorded in the giver's books and records, provided only to reflect esteem or gratitude, and permitted under local law. Items of nominal value, such as cab fare, reasonable meals and entertainment expenses, or company promotional items, are unlikely to improperly influence an official, and, as a result, are not, by themselves, items that have resulted in enforcement action by the government. But be careful. An attempt to hide what is really a bribe to a foreign official under the guise of making a charitable donation can land you in hot water. Is it really a bona fide charity? Or instead, is it just a way of funneling money to the foreign official?

Let's add a few words about payments made to foreign "consultants" or other intermediaries. Especially for those in accounting and finance, know that oftentimes these consultants may not be anything more than conduits for cash to be funneled to a foreign official. Look for certain "red flags" or warning signs that something may not be quite right. For example, do you see unusual payment patters or strange financial arrangements with the consultant? Is there a history of corruption in the country in question? Is the intermediary unwilling to certify that he will not be bribing anyone? Are there unusually high commissions being paid? Are expense reports vague or incomplete? Does the consultant really have no qualifications for the job? Did a foreign official recommend the intermediary to your company? The more of this you see the more you should be on guard that something is amiss.

The fifth and last test is that the payment must be made, or offered to a foreign official. The FCPA defines "foreign official" to include: any officer or employee of a foreign government or any department, agency, or instrumentality thereof, or of a public international organization, or any person acting in an official capacity for or on behalf of any such government or department, agency, or instrumentality, or for or on behalf of any such public international organization. This also includes an official of a foreign political party or any candidate running for a foreign political office.

So what happens if the government accuses you of violating the Act? You have some defenses you can raise, which if you can prove, you are off the hook. The first defense

---

6 IBID p. 14

is that the payment you made was legal under the written laws of the foreign country in question. This is the so-called "local law" defense. Let's look at this closely. You may conclude that making certain payments to foreign officials in a certain country is a common practice. Even if true, that doesn't help you. You have to show that there are specific *written* laws authorizing those payments. If you can find those laws, which is not very likely, then you are safe.

The second defense is the so called "reasonable and bona fide business expenditure" defense. The FCPA allows companies to provide reasonable and bona fide travel and lodging expenses to a foreign official. Additionally, expenses paid that are directly related to the promotion, demonstration, or explanation of a company's products or services, or are related to a company's execution or performance of a contract with a foreign government or agency are also allowed. Note, however, trips that are primarily for personal entertainment purposes are not bona fide business expenses and may violate the FCPA's anti-bribery provisions.

There is another category of payments that a company can make which on their face, you would think would violate that Act. However, the government has said that these so called "facilitating payments" are allowed. These are payments made only to facilitate or expedite routine government actions. Examples of "routine governmental actions" ordinarily performed by a foreign official include actions such as the following:

- obtaining permits, licenses, or other official documents to qualify a person to do business in a foreign country;
- processing governmental papers, such as visas and work orders;
- providing police protection, mail pickup and delivery, or scheduling inspections associated with contract performance or inspections related to transit of goods across country;
- providing phone service, power and water supply, loading and unloading cargo, or protecting perishable products or commodities from deterioration; or
- actions of a similar nature.[7]

So what can happen to you if you violate the FCPA? A lot of things can happen, and none of them any good. First, the business can be fined up to $2,000,000, and in some cases more. Officers, directors, agents, employees and even shareholders can be individually fined up to $100,000 and sentenced up to five years in prison. Additionally, the company can be barred from doing any business with the U.S. Government. The obvious best advice, stay away from bribing foreign officials. Not only is it morally wrong, but as you can see, it can have catastrophic legal consequences.

9.4 INTER-COMPANY BRIBES

You are CEO of a large American company. Your sales manager has been working on a large multi-million dollar contract with a foreign company. Although you are the only U.S. company involved in the bidding, you have lots of international competition for the contract. Your manager comes to you and gives you the status of the negotiations. Your

---

7 IBID p. 25

product and price look very good in comparison to the competition. However, there is one problem. The procurement agent for the potential buyer has made it known that if your company wants a real chance at winning the contract, a deposit of $100,000 must be made to his private Swiss bank account. You also know that your competitors have already made such transfers. Your sales manager urges you to make the payment. He feels that if this hurdle is overcome, based on the quality and price of your product, you have a very good chance of getting the deal. He puts it to you this way. "I can't guarantee that if we make the payment we will get the deal. I can guarantee, however, that if we do not make the payment we will absolutely not get the deal." He sees that you are a bit uncomfortable with this and quickly adds that you should not worry because first, this does not violate the Foreign Corrupt Practices Act as no government official is involved and second, everyone else is doing it. So do you want a chance at the deal or not? What would you do?

Now is a good time to review the process of decision making that we talked about in Chapter Four. Let's do this by the numbers.

Step one: Do we understand the objective facts of the problem? Presuming that what our sales manager has told us is true, it appears that there is little disagreement about the facts of the situation.

Step two: What exactly are the ethical problems that you are facing? In the case at hand, what is the dilemma? It seems that you either pay the bribe, and that's what this really is, or not. If you do pay it, arguably the company could land a significant contract, which works to the benefit of the company as well as its shareholders. Of course in doing so, you might be violating some core ethical principles of your company, not to speak of your own personal principles. If you do not pay, then have you done harm to both the company and its shareholders?

Is there a legal issue? Is there a regulatory conflict? For example, legally, just because you may not be violating the FCPA does not mean that you are not in violation of other laws, including the laws of the foreign country. The same may be true for regulatory problems.

Is there a professional or corporate issue? Very likely there is. If you take a look at the mission statement of your company, the chances are very good that somewhere in that statement is something about conducting your business only in accordance with the highest of ethical standards. (If your mission statement doesn't say this, it's time to go back and rewrite that statement.) More so, even apart from the mission statement, if you, as CEO, were asked what kind of business you want to run, what kind of business you want others to see you as, how would you answer? Would you be happy saying that your company is one that puts profits over everything, including basic standards of morality? Probably not.

What about industry standards? Is the paying of inter-company bribes an accepted practice in the industry? This may not be so obvious of a problem. We would like to think that of course, this sort of activity runs contrary to the standards of the industry. But what if it doesn't? In other words, what if in a given business inter-company bribes are in fact a common practice? This goes to our sales manager saying, "Everyone does it." As you might remember from our discussions regarding rationalizations, you may have answered your own question. If you have to go to rationalizing the conduct, you are admitting, even if not publicly, that the conduct is wrong. Now you have to decide to either do what you already know is wrong or not.

Step three: Identify all those who may be affected by the issue and the decisions that you make regarding the issue. As we all know by now, no decision takes place in a vacuum. Who are all of the parties that might be affected by whatever decisions you make? First there are the shareholders. If you pay the bribe and get the business, they may realize a gain. However, what might their reaction be if they knew that you paid a bribe to get the business? Experience tells us that most shareholders would not find this acceptable. And worse, what happens if you pay the bribe and do not get the business? It may be safe to say that you should start looking for a new job. What of your managers and employees? If you pay the bribe you are setting a tone from the top that says this sort of conduct is acceptable. Are you sure that you want to surround yourself with employees who believe it is alright to bribe and by extension engage in other conduct that is morally questionable? Most CEOs would not. What about your vendors? If word gets out that you pay bribes to obtain business are you not telling them that if they want to do business with you a bribe or two paid by them to you would go a long way in solidifying their relationship with your company? Is that the message you want? What of the local community? Companies spend a lot of money trying to show that they are good citizens in the community in which they reside. If you pay the bribe, what do you think the reaction would be if that fact became the headline story in the local community newspaper? One other point to remember. If you pay the bribe you may fall into the "blackmailer" dilemma. That is, once you pay a blackmailer, he never goes away. He will always come back for more money. Once you set a precedent that you pay business bribes, do not be surprised if this problem comes up over and over again in your company's future. If you analyze all of these factors, do you still think that it is a good idea to pay the bribe?

Step four: What are your options? On its face it looks like you only have two choices: pay the bribe or not. But is this really true? Remember back in Chapter Two we talked about logical fallacies. One of them was the fallacy of the false dichotomy, the false choice. Are there other ways that you can influence the decision maker of the foreign company besides paying him a bribe? Never underestimate the power of honest persuasion. Could you take the issue of the bribe head on, and tell the foreign corporate official that your company does not do business that way, and remind him of his duty to buy the best product for his company's needs, which of course you will argue is yours. Do you play some hardball and tell that foreign corporate official that you want to confirm his "business practice" by talking to his corporate superior? Perhaps you can come up with other options as well.

Step five: Make a decision. This step speaks for itself. Remember that whatever you decide is going to determine and speak to the person that you are, hope to be, and the company you work for. The choice is yours.

Unfortunately there is no getting around the problem of international bribery in business. One of the criticisms of the Foreign Corrupt Practices Act, for instance, is that it makes U.S. companies less competitive with their foreign competitors who are not constrained by such laws in their own countries. As for inter-company pay-offs, was your sales manager possibly correct in saying that everyone else was doing it? Maybe so. But for all the reasons given above, both ethical and legal, you have a duty to not participate in such activities. Does this mean that sometimes you may not get the deal? Yes, it does. However, over time the reputation of your company, as well as your personal reputation for engaging in only honest business dealings and integrity will come out far ahead in the long run.

9.5 CHAPTER HIGHLIGHTS

1. What are the two most common types of bribes that one may encounter in international dealings?

They are bribery of foreign officials and inter-company bribes.

2. What is the purpose of the Foreign Corrupt Practices Act?

The Act was intended to halt corrupt practices, create a level playing field for honest businesses, and restore public confidence in the integrity of the marketplace.

3. In general, what does the FCPA prohibit?

The FCPA prohibits offering to pay, paying, promising to pay, or authorizing the payment of money or anything of value to a foreign official in order to influence any act or decision of the foreign official in his or her official capacity or to secure any other improper advantage in order to obtain or retain business.

4. What are the five tests the government must pass to hold you and/or your company liable for violating the FCPA?

They are the following: jurisdiction, or the "who" test, the business purpose test or the "what" test, the corrupt intent test, the payment test, the foreign official test.

5. What are the red flags that you should watch out for when dealing with foreign consultants or intermediaries?

Do you see unusual payment patters or strange financial arrangements with the consultant? Is there a history of corruption in the country in question? Is the intermediary unwilling to certify that he will not be bribing anyone? Are there unusually high commissions being paid? Are expense reports vague or incomplete? Does the consultant really have no qualifications for the job? Was the intermediary recommended to your company by a foreign official?

6. What are two defenses that you can raise if accused of violating the FCPA?

The local law defense and the reasonable and bona fide business expenditure defense are the two defenses.

7. What are "facilitating payments?"

These are payments made only to facilitate or expedite routine government actions.

9.6 PROBLEM FOR DISCUSSION

Megacorp is a large multi-national mining company with operations in Foreign Country, where it recently identified a significant new ore deposit. It has ready buyers for the new ore but has limited capacity to get it to market. In order to increase the size and speed of its ore export, Megacorp will need to build a new road from its facility to the port that can accommodate larger trucks. Megacorp retains an agent in Foreign Country to assist it in obtaining the required permits, including an environmental permit, to build the road. The agent informs Megacorp's vice president for international operations that he plans to make a one-time small cash payment to a clerk in the relevant government office to ensure that the clerk files and stamps the permit applications expeditiously, as the agent has experienced delays of three months when he has not made this "grease" payment. The clerk has no discretion about whether to file and stamp the permit applications once the requisite filing fee has been paid. The vice president authorizes the payment. A few months later, the agent tells the vice president that he has run into a problem obtaining a necessary environmental permit. It turns out that the planned road construction would adversely impact an environmentally sensitive and protected local wetland. While the problem could be overcome by rerouting the road, such rerouting would cost Megacorp $1 million more and would slow down construction by six months. It would also increase the transit time for the ore and reduce the number of monthly shipments. The agent tells the vice president that he is a good friend with the director of Foreign Country's Department of Natural Resources and that it would only take a modest cash payment to the director and the "problem would go away." The vice president authorizes the payment, and the agent makes it. After receiving the payment, the director issues the permit, and Megacorp constructs its new road through the wetlands.[1]

- What problems do you see in the above example?
- If in fact the payments in both cases were considered normal business practices in the Foreign County, how would you answer?

---

1   IBID p 26